JOHN

BOOKS OF FAITH SERIES
Leader Session Guide

Susan M. Lang

AUGSBURG FORTRESS
Minneapolis

JOHN
Leader Session Guide

Books of Faith Series
Book of Faith Adult Bible Studies

This Leader Session Guide is also available for purchase online at www.augsburgfortress.org.

Copyright © 2009 Augsburg Fortress. All rights reserved. Except for brief quotations in critical articles or reviews, no part of this book may be reproduced in any manner without prior written permission from the publisher. For more information, visit: www.augsburgfortress.org/copyrights or write to: Permissions, Augsburg Fortress, Box 1209, Minneapolis, MN 55440-1209.

 Book of Faith is an initiative of the
Evangelical Lutheran Church in America
God's work. Our hands.

For more information about the Book of Faith initiative, go to www.bookoffaith.org.

Scripture quotations, unless otherwise marked, are from New Revised Standard Version Bible, copyright © 1989 Division of Christian Education of the National Council of Churches of Christ in the United States of America. Used by permission. All rights reserved.

Image acknowledgments: illustration on pg. 55 copyright © 2003 Augsburg Fortress; all other images (as indicated) copyright © SuperStock. All rights reserved.

ISBN: 978-0-8066-9589-1
Writer: Susan M. Lang
Cover and interior design: Spunk Design Machine, spkdm.com
Typesetting: PerfecType, Nashville, TN

The paper used in this publication meets the minimum requirements of American National Standard for Information Sciences—Permanence of Paper for Printed Library Materials, ANSI Z329.48-1984.

Manufactured in the U.S.A.
13 12 11 10 09   1 2 3 4 5 6 7 8 9 10

CONTENTS

	Introduction	5
1	What Is Jesus' Relationship with God? *John 1:1-18*	9
2	How Is It Possible for Us to Be in Relationship with God? *John 3:1-21*	19
3	What Does It Mean that Jesus Is the "Bread of Life"? *John 6:25-59*	29
4	Who Can See Jesus? *John 9:1-41*	39
5	What Does It Mean that Jesus Is the "Resurrection and the Life"? *John 11:1-44*	47
6	What Does It Mean to Be a Disciple of Jesus? *John 13:1-35*	55
7	How Does Jesus Want His Disciples to Relate to the World? *John 17:1-26*	63
8	How Does Jesus' Relationship with His Disciples Continue? *John 20:11-31*	73

Introduction

Book of Faith Adult Bible Studies

Welcome to the conversation! The Bible study resources you are using are created to support the bold vision of the Book of Faith initiative that calls "the whole church to become more fluent in the first language of faith, the language of Scripture, in order that we might live into our calling as a people renewed, enlivened, empowered, and sent by the Word."

Simply put, this initiative and these resources invite you to "Open Scripture. Join the Conversation."

We enter into this conversation based on the promise that exploring the Bible deeply with others opens us to God working in and through us. God's Word is life changing, church changing, and world changing. Lutheran approaches to Scripture provide a fruitful foundation for connecting Bible, life, and faith.

A Session Overview

Each session is divided into the following four key sections. The amount of time spent in each section may vary based on choices you make. The core Learner Session Guide is designed for 50 minutes. A session can be expanded to as much as 90 minutes by using the Bonus Activities that appear in the Leader Session Guide.

- **Gather (10-15 minutes)**

Time to check in, make introductions, review homework assignments, share an opening prayer, and use the Focus Activity to introduce learners to the Session Focus.

- **Open Scripture (10-15 minutes)**

The session Scripture text is read using a variety of methods and activities. Learners are asked to respond to a few general questions. As leader, you may want to capture initial thoughts or questions on paper for later review.

- **Join the Conversation (25-55 minutes)**

Learners explore the session Scripture text through core questions and activities that cover each of the four perspectives (see diagram on p. 6). The core Learner Session Guide material may be expanded through use of the Bonus Activities provided in the Leader Session Guide. Each session ends with a brief Wrap-Up and prayer.

- **Extending the Conversation (5 minutes)**

Lists homework assignments, including next week's session Scripture text. The leader may choose one or more items to assign for all. Each session also includes additional Enrichment options and may include For Further Reading suggestions.

A Method to Guide the Conversation

Book of Faith Adult Bible Studies has three primary goals:

- To increase biblical fluency;
- To encourage and facilitate informed small group conversation based on God's Word; and
- To renew and empower us to carry out God's mission for the sake of the world.

To accomplish these goals, each session will explore one or more primary Bible texts from four different angles and contexts—historical, literary, Lutheran, and devotional. These particular ways of exploring a text are not new, but used in combination they provide a full understanding of and experience with the text.

Complementing this approach is a commitment to engaging participants in active, learner-orientated Bible conversations. The resources call for prepared leaders to facilitate learner discovery, discussion, and activity. Active learning and frequent engagement with Scripture will lead to greater biblical fluency and encourage active faith.

1 We begin by reading the Bible text and reflecting on its meaning. We ask questions and identify items that are unclear. We bring our unique background and experience to the Bible, and the Bible meets us where we are.

5 We return to where we started, but now we have explored and experienced the Bible text from four different dimensions. We are ready to move into the "for" dimension. We have opened Scripture and joined in conversation for a purpose. We consider the meaning of the text for faithful living. We wonder what God is calling us (individually and as communities of faith) to do. We consider how God's Word is calling us to do God's work in the world.

2* We seek to understand the world of the Bible and locate the setting of the text. We explore who may have written the text and why. We seek to understand the particular social and cultural contexts that influenced the content and the message. We wonder who the original audience may have been. We think about how these things "translate" to our world today.

4 We consider the Lutheran principles that help ground our interpretation of the Bible text. We ask questions that bring those principles and unique Lutheran theological insights into conversation with the text. We discover how our Lutheran insights can ground and focus our understanding and shape our faithful response to the text.

3* We pay close attention to how the text is written. We notice what kind of literature it is and how this type of literature may function or may be used. We look at the characters, the story line, and the themes. We compare and contrast these with our own understanding and experience of life. In this interchange, we discover meaning.

- Devotional Context
- Historical Context
- Lutheran Context
- Literary Context

* Sessions may begin with either Historical Context or Literary Context.

The diagram on p. 6 summarizes the general way this method is intended to work. A more detailed introduction to the method used in Book of Faith Adult Bible Studies is available in *Opening the Book of Faith* (Augsburg Fortress, 2008).

The Learner Session Guide

The Learner Session Guide content is built on the four sections (see p. 5). The content included in the main "Join the Conversation" section is considered to be the core material needed to explore the session Scripture text. Each session includes a Focus Image that is used as part of an activity or question somewhere within the core session. Other visuals (maps, charts, photographs, and illustrations) may be included to help enhance the learner's experience with the text and its key concepts.

For those subscribing to the Web version of Book of Faith Adult Bible Studies, the Learner Session Guides will be downloaded and printed in preparation for the session, or they may simply be projected for groups that decide to be paperless.

The Leader Session Guide

For easy reference, the Leader Session Guide contains all the content included in the Learner Session Guide and more. The elements that are unique to the Leader Session Guide are the following:

- **Before You Begin**—Helpful tips to use as you prepare to lead the session.
- **Session Overview**—Contains detailed description of key themes and content covered in each of the four contexts (Historical, Literary, Lutheran, Devotional). Core questions and activities in the Learner Session Guide are intended to emerge directly from this Session Overview. Highlighted parts of the Session Overview provide a kind of "quick prep" for those wanting to do an initial scan of the key session themes and content.
- **Key Definitions**—Key terms or concepts that appear in the Session Overview may be illustrated or defined.
- **Facilitator's Prayer**—To help the leader center on the session theme and leadership task.
- **Bonus Activities**—Optional activities included in each of the four sections of "Join the Conversation" used by the leader to expand the core session.
- **Tips**—A variety of helpful hints, instructions, or background content to aid leadership facilitation.
- **Looking Ahead**—Reminders to the leader about preparation for the upcoming session.

Session Prep Video

(Available on the DVD that accompanies this unit.) To help you prepare to lead the session, Session Prep Video segments have been created. A guide will walk with you through a session overview and the key parts of the session flow. These segments can provide helpful hints, but they are not meant to replace your own deeper preparation.

Leader and Learner

In Book of Faith Adult Bible Studies, the leader's primary task is facilitating small group conversation and activity. These conversations are built around structured learning tasks. What is a structured learning task? It is an open question or activity that engages learners with new content and the resources they need to respond. Underlying this structured dialog approach are three primary assumptions about adult learners:

- Adult learners bring with them varied experiences and the capability to do active learning tasks;
- Adult learners learn best when they are invited to be actively involved in learning; and
- Adults are more accountable and engaged when active learning tasks are used.

Simply put, the goal is fluency in the first language of faith, the language of Scripture. How does one become fluent in a new language, proficient in building houses, or skilled at hitting a baseball? By practicing and doing in a hands-on way. Book of Faith Adult Bible Studies provides the kind of hands-on Bible exploration that will produce Bible-fluent learners equipped to do God's work in the world.

Books of Faith Series

Book of Faith Adult Bible Studies includes several series and courses. This John unit is part of the Books of Faith Series, which is designed to explore key themes and texts in the books of the Bible. Each book of the Bible reveals a unique story or message of faith. Many core themes, story lines, and characters are shared by several books, but each book in its own right is a book of faith. Exploring these books of faith in depth opens us to the variety and richness of God's written word for us.

John Unit Overview

When you read the Gospel of John, you are immediately struck by its poetic quality and the prevalence of imagery and metaphor that is not present in the Gospels of Matthew, Mark, or Luke.

The Gospel of John begins by taking a cosmic approach that shows us the depth of Jesus' relationship to God. Jesus is the Incarnate Word, united with God even before creation. This is an important theme that runs throughout the Gospel. According to John, disciples of Christ know God and have a relationship with God because of their belief in Jesus.

John's uniqueness as a book of faith is highlighted by other major themes that differentiate this Gospel from the Gospels of Matthew, Mark, and Luke:

In the other Gospels, Jesus uses parables in his teaching, but parables are absent in John. Instead you'll find long theological discourses (see John 3:1-21; 6:22-71; 10:1-21; 12:27-50; 14:1—17:26).

John's Gospel makes use of "I am" statements in which Jesus articulates his true identity in word pictures or images meant to speak directly to the people. The "I am" images he uses include the bread of life, the light of the world, the good shepherd, the resurrection and the life, and the true vine.

Instead of speaking about the kingdom of God, John's Gospel shows how believing in Jesus as God's Incarnate Word gives us eternal life, both now and for all time. Believing in the Son radically connects us to God. This connection transcends time and space.

Session 1, What Is Jesus' Relationship with God? (John 1:1-18), explores Jesus' incarnation and relationship with God even before creation.

Session 2, How Is It Possible for Us to Be in Relationship with God? (John 3:1-21), looks at Jesus' role in our lives and in our relationship with God. Through Jesus, God's gift of love to the world, we receive new life and live in God's presence forever.

Session 3, What Does It Mean that Jesus Is the "Bread of Life"? (John 6:25-59), offers a deeper look at one of Jesus' "I am" sayings. When we share the "bread of life" in the Eucharist, we share in Jesus' life, death, and resurrection.

Session 4, Who Can See Jesus? (John 9:1-41), shows that it takes faith to see Jesus.

Session 5, What Does It Mean that Jesus Is the "Resurrection and the Life"? (John 11:1-44), focuses on Jesus' power over life and death, now and for all time.

Session 6, What Does It Mean to Be a Disciple of Jesus? (John 13:1-35), explores Jesus' command to love one another. Through love and service to our neighbor, we are recognized as Jesus' disciples.

Session 7, How Does Jesus Want His Disciples to Relate to the World? (John 17:1-26), shows that Jesus unites us with God and with one another, and sends us out to continue his ministry in the world.

Session 8, How Does Jesus' Relationship with His Disciples Continue? (John 20:11-31), explores the gift of the Holy Spirit, who accompanies us as we go forth in Jesus' name.

SESSION ONE

John 1:1-18

Leader Session Guide

Focus Statement
We see and experience God through Jesus, the Incarnate Word, one with God even before creation.

Key Verse
And the Word became flesh and lived among us, and we have seen his glory, the glory as of a father's only son, full of grace and truth. John 1:14

Focus Image

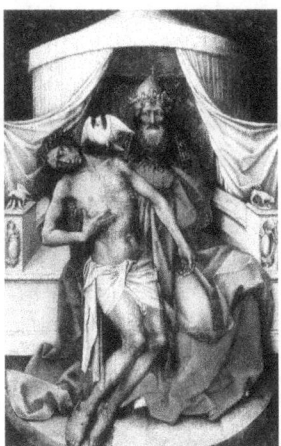

The Trinity (Father, Son and the Holy Ghost as a dove). Left wing of a triptych. Robert Campin (1378-1444).
© Image Asset Mgmt Ltd. / SuperStock

What Is Jesus' Relationship with God?

Session Preparation

Before You Begin...
Take time to reflect upon what it means to you that Jesus, the Incarnate Word—God's Word made flesh—existed before time itself. What effect does this have on your relationship with Jesus?

Session Instructions

1. View the Session Prep Video.

2. Take time to read this Leader Session Guide and mark the activities you intend to include in your group session. What points do you plan to emphasize? Highlight them.

3. Review all activities, checking for necessary materials. Collect these prior to the session.

4. Have extra Bibles on hand in case a member of the group forgets to bring one.

Session Overview

There are four Gospels in the Bible that tell the good news of Jesus Christ: Matthew, Mark, Luke, and John. The first three are called the **Synoptic** Gospels because they share the same view and similar or overlapping stories. John's Gospel, however, is very different in writing and approach. It opens with a cosmic approach that speaks of Jesus' presence and relationship with God even before the beginning of time and creation. The significance of the depth of this relationship is an important theme that runs through the entire book. It also has a deeper meaning for Jesus' disciples. Through him, they too are intimately connected with God. Keep this theme in mind as your group studies the Gospel of John. Look for the many ways in which it appears throughout this book of faith.

HISTORICAL CONTEXT

The author of the Gospel of John was traditionally believed to be Jesus' disciple, John the son of Zebedee. However, many now believe that the author was a member of a Christian community in Asia Minor, possibly founded by the "beloved disciple" mentioned in the Gospel of John. The tensions between followers of Jesus and Jewish religious leaders are portrayed throughout the Gospel. Some scholars believe this indicates that John was written

Session 1: John 1:1-18

SESSION ONE

? Synoptic:
"Seeing together" or having a common perspective (from the Greek *syn* meaning "together" and *optic* related to "seeing").

? Synagogues:
Jewish places of worship.

? Prologue:
Introduction, preface, or opening (seen as verses 1-18 in John 1).

? Deuterocanonical books / Apocrypha:
Books not included in either the Jewish or Protestant canon (meaning "accepted list" of books). These books, also known as the Apocrypha, are accepted and listed as canon by many Christians. Roman Catholics and Orthodox Christians include many of these books in their accepted canons.

after Christians were expelled from the **synagogues** around 90 C.E. Whether or not this is the case is debated, but it does appear tensions were high between Jewish leaders and Jewish Christians when John's Gospel was written. This situation plays an important role in John. In none of the other Gospels are "the Jews" identified as frequently, especially in opposition to Jesus and his followers.

Yet, the Christians of John's time clearly see themselves in a continuous line with Israel and its history and faith story. (The insight that the Christians of John's community celebrated their Jewish lineage is an important one in light of the fact that some readers have interpreted the Gospel of John as anti-Semitic.) Your group will explore how both realities are demonstrated in the **prologue** of the Gospel of John, especially John 1:17, which demonstrates the link between Moses and Jesus.

LITERARY CONTEXT

John's prologue raises several themes that will continue throughout the Gospel: light and darkness, belief, truth, witness, and the identity of Jesus. Your group will begin to identify these themes and the relationship between the Word and God.

Your group will also explore similar themes in John and Wisdom literature of the Old Testament. You'll see that Wisdom is intimately connected with God and is even present at creation (Proverbs 8:22-36). The Wisdom of Solomon, one of the **Deuterocanonical books**, also known as the **Apocrypha**, describes Wisdom as the "breath of the power of God, and a pure emanation of the glory of the Almighty" (Wisdom of Solomon 7:25). The descriptions of Wisdom are similar to the description of the Word in the Gospel of John. Both Wisdom and the Word are present at creation. However, Wisdom in the Old Testament is personified as a woman and is not equated with God in the same way that the Word is. In the Old Testament, Wisdom serves God. You'll look at the similarities and differences between Wisdom and the Word that became flesh to communicate God's love.

LUTHERAN CONTEXT

The Gospel of John and the first creation story in Genesis both start with the same words: "In the beginning." Your group will use Luther's principle of "Scripture interprets Scripture" to examine several texts, including Genesis 1:1—2:4 and Colossians 1:15-23, that will shed light on the meaning of John's prologue. Both Genesis and the prologue of John start with a more expansive, cosmic view of creation. Genesis also shows us the creative power of God's spoken Word. God speaks and the world and all living things come into being. In John's Gospel, the Word becomes flesh, walks among us, and ushers in a new creation in which God is now intimately connected to humanity in an incredibly powerful way. Colossians 1:15-23 also speaks of Jesus' existence before creation and how through him we are reconciled with God.

Another text that may be helpful as you discuss John's prologue is 1 John 1:1—2:2. Notice the similarity in use of language and imagery. The passage in 1 John also focuses on Jesus' identity as both divine and human.

Devotional Context

What is Jesus' real relationship with God? What does that mean for us? These two questions are at the heart of approaching this text from a devotional perspective. From the beginning of the Gospel, John clearly places Jesus in a deep and highly connected relationship with God. Jesus refers to the depth of this relationship throughout the Gospel when he speaks both of being sent by and being of one mind with God. He also speaks of himself as being the "gate" through which the sheep must pass to have an abundant life in God (John 5:22-23; 6:44; 6:57; 10:7; 10:30; 14:6-7).

God speaks to us profoundly when the Word takes on flesh and a human life. Group members will explore what it means to them that Jesus is the Incarnate Word of God. How have they experienced Jesus' **incarnation** in their lives in real and "fleshy" ways? How does God speak to them through those they encounter daily?

 Incarnation: Personification, embodiment, materialization; term used by Christians to describe God's Word taking on flesh in Jesus.

The immensity of God's love for us cannot be overstated when reading this text. The Word became flesh in order to enter into a deeper communion with us so that we, too, might know God as Jesus does.

Facilitator's Prayer

Before participants arrive, find a quiet place and pray:

O Word made flesh, sometimes it is hard to feel your presence as I rush through my busy and often hectic schedule. Quiet both my heart and mind as I prepare to lead. Empower me to feel your presence through the conversation and participation of all those in the room so that, together, we might come to know you better. Amen.

SESSION ONE

Tip:
Start your session with introductions. If you are seated around a table, give each person an index card. Have participants make name cards by folding the index cards in half (joining the shorter edges together), writing their names on the cards, and placing the cards on the table in front of them. Use these cards each week until group members are familiar with each other. You could also use name tags.

Tip:
The Focus Activity will help learners begin to think about the relationship between words and actions as you launch your study on the Word made flesh. Have learners break into trios for discussion. After a few minutes, gather in the large group again to share reflections.

Tip:
If you choose to use a candle, check your local fire codes and your congregation's fire polices regarding the use of open flames.

Tip:
Ask group members about their hopes and expectations for studying the Gospel of John. Studying the Bible can raise anxiety for participants who may feel their knowledge is inadequate. Assure them that they will all experience new insights. Encourage sharing.

Tip:
Also be aware that some learners may initially feel uncomfortable in a large group setting. Assure everyone that they need only share the things they feel comfortable sharing.

Gather (10-15 minutes)

Check-in
Take time to connect or reconnect with the others in your group.

Pray
God of love,
You sent your son Jesus into the world. He is your Word to us, now and for all time. Thank you for speaking to us through him, and also through Scripture and through one another. In Jesus' name. Amen.

Focus Activity
Discuss the meaning of the phrase "actions speak louder than words." Tell how you have experienced this in your life. Have words ever been louder than actions?

Open Scripture (10-15 minutes)

Read John 1:1-18.
- What verse did you most connect with as the text was read?
- What are the key images?
- What did you find intriguing or confusing?

Here are options for introducing the text:
- Light a candle before reading the text. Dim the room lights, if possible.
- Invite two group members to read the text, one at a time. Give some time for quiet reflection in between the readings. (Asking the two people prior to the session will give them an opportunity to practice either a meditative or dramatic reading.)

Join the Conversation (25-55 minutes)

Historical Context
The earliest Christians came from the Jewish faith and still clung to their Jewish identity. They believed Jesus was the promised Messiah and, therefore, he continued the history and faith of Israel. There is evidence, however, that tensions between Jewish

Christians and Jewish religious leaders increased after the destruction of the temple in 70 C.E. There may have been a formal decree that eventually expelled the Jewish followers of Jesus from the synagogue, the Jewish place of worship. It does appear that tensions were high when John's Gospel was written. Keep this in mind as you study the Gospel.

1. Where in the session Scripture text do you see any kind of conflict? Is it a conflict in values, belief, decisions, or actions? Who is involved?

2. What evidence do you see in the text that the Christians of John's community saw themselves in line with the history and faith of Israel?

Literary Context

1. The Gospel of John doesn't begin with a story about Mary, Joseph, Bethlehem, shepherds, a star, or Wise Men. It begins instead with a "prologue" or introduction in John 1:1-18. This introduction (which is also the session Scripture text) raises themes that will continue to be important throughout the Gospel.

- List key words and themes that appear in the text.
- How is the Word's relationship to God described?
- If you were writing a book about Jesus, where or how would you begin?

2. The books in the New Testament were originally written in Greek. The Greek term for "word" is *logos* (LOW-gohs), derived from the plan giving order to the universe in Greek thought, as well as divine Wisdom in Judaism. Many scholars see a correlation between Wisdom personified in the Old Testament and the Deuterocanon/Apocrypha (books not included in the Jewish or Protestant canon or "accepted list" of biblical books) and the Word made flesh or Incarnate Word in John's prologue. Wisdom and the Word are both said to be present at creation, although only in John is the Word equated with God.

Read Proverbs 8:22-36 and the following passage from a deuterocanonical book written in praise of Wisdom:

> For she is a breath of the power of God, and a pure emanation of the glory of the Almighty; therefore nothing defiled gains entrance into her. Wisdom of Solomon 7:25

- What do these passages say about Wisdom.
- Compare this to what John 1:1-18 says about the Word.

Bonus Activity:
Break into smaller groups. Use commentaries and study Bibles to look up some historical background on the text. What were the conditions and conflicts thought to be in effect during the writing of John's Gospel? How might these have affected John's writing?

Bonus Activity:
Reflect and write down your thoughts about how Christianity might be in conflict with the norms of our society. What correlations might that have for the Christians of John's time?

Bonus Activity:
Sing or read the words to hymn 514, 518, or 648 in *Evangelical Lutheran Worship*. All of these hymns mention Wisdom in relationship to Christ. What do these hymns say to you?

Bonus Activity:
Select volunteers to read both the Proverbs text and John 1:14 from two different Bible translations. What new insights does the group have as a result of hearing the variations in the texts? Chart some of the differences the group notices.

SESSION ONE

Bonus Activity:
Distribute paper and pens to the group. Break into pairs or trios. Instruct learners to list words and ideas found in both John 1:1-18 and Colossians 1:15-23. Now draw connections between the two texts. What new insights are drawn out by this activity?

Tip:
Distribute paper and pens to the group. Break into pairs or trios. Instruct learners to list words and ideas found in the three statements and John 1:1-18. Now draw connections between these. What new insights are drawn out by this activity?

Bonus Activity:
Purchase small notebooks for participants to use as journals during the sessions. After your discussion, ask them to journal their thoughts on what it means to them that Jesus, the Incarnate Word of God, existed before time itself. What effect does this have on their relationship with Jesus?

Bonus Activity:
Distribute lumps of clay to participants and ask them to sculpt representations of what John 1:1-18 means for them in their lives.

Lutheran Context

1. Using the Lutheran principle of Scripture interprets Scripture, look at other Bible passages that help interpret the session Scripture text. Read Genesis 1:1—2:4 and Colossians 1:15-23, then discuss the questions.

- How is God's Word present and active in the Genesis story?
- List themes that you find in both texts.

2. The Confession of Faith of the Evangelical Lutheran Church in America (ELCA) states that the Word of God speaks to us in three ways:

> 2.02.a. Jesus Christ is the Word of God incarnate, through whom everything was made and through whose life, death, and resurrection God fashions a new creation.

> b. The proclamation of God's message to us as both Law and Gospel is the Word of God, revealing judgment and mercy through word and deed, beginning with the Word in creation, continuing in the history of Israel, and centering in all its fullness in the person and work of Jesus Christ.

> c. The canonical Scriptures of the Old and New Testaments are the written Word of God. Inspired by God's Spirit speaking through their authors, they record and announce God's revelation centering in Jesus Christ. Through them God's Spirit speaks to us to create and sustain Christian faith and fellowship for service in the world.

- Compare these three statements with John 1:1-18 and list the similarities.

Devotional Context

1. God's Word speaks through Jesus Christ, through believers, and through the Bible.

- Give an example of the Word speaking to you or your congregation in one of these ways.
- God's Word can speak through you. What do you think about that?

2. Look back at the Focus Image at the start of the session. This is one artist's picture of the relationship between God and Jesus (and the Holy Spirit as well). Draw a picture or describe how you see the relationship between God and Jesus.

- How have you seen Jesus "in the flesh" in your life? How does God speak to you through the people you encounter each day?

Wrap-up

Be ready to look back over the work your group has done in this session.

1. Refer back to the group's hopes and expectations for studying John, and ask if any of these were met in this session. As a result of this session, are there any additional hopes and expectations for your future time together?

2. Ask group members what the highlight of the session was for them. What did they find most engaging and why? Take note of the responses as you plan future sessions. Especially take note of the types of activities the group seems to enjoy.

3. Point out any "ah-ha" moments that you noticed in the session. Thank group members for their openness and willingness to participate. The more comfortable the group becomes, the more open they will become in sharing, and you'll have many more "ah-has" to come.

4. Point out the homework in Extending the Conversation and invite group members to select assignments that particularly appeal to them. Review these at the start of the next session.

Tip: Check in with everyone during this time. How are participants feeling about today's session? Do they have recommendations for your next time together?

Tip: Monitor the mood of the participants. Does everyone seem comfortable with what transpired in the session? If not, check in privately with those exhibiting any uneasiness. This may or may not be related to the session.

Pray

O Loving God, we thank you that you concretely spoke and showed us the depth of your love for us by sending your Son Jesus Christ, the Incarnate Word, to live and dwell among us. We give you thanks that through him we can come to know your truth and grace more fully and participate in a deeper relationship with you. Help us to live our lives in celebration of the Word made flesh by sharing your word, love, and grace with friends, family, and strangers alike. In Jesus' name we pray. Amen.

Extending the Conversation (5 minutes)

Homework

1. Read the Scripture text for the next session: John 3:1-21. If time permits, read all of John 1:1—3:21 (see page 18 for a daily reading plan).

2. During the course of the week, meditate on John 1:1-18. If you develop any new insights or thoughts, jot them down to share next week.

Tip: Encourage participants to bring any homework that they do to the next session to share with others in the group.

SESSION ONE

3. Use John 1:1-18 as inspiration for writing a hymn. Start by picking a favorite hymn tune and then write lyrics to fit the music.

4. Take photographs or capture images and then create your own visual presentation on the meaning of John 1:1-18.

Looking Ahead

1. Reflect on how things went during this session. What did you learn about facilitating a Bible study? What worked well? What might you have done differently?

2. Reflect upon the preferred learning styles of your adult learners. What came easier to your group? Do they prefer learning through visual means, conversational means, or through physical activities?

3. Read the Scripture text for the next session: John 3:1-21.

4. Read through the Leader Guide for the next session and mark portions you wish to highlight for the group.

5. Make a checklist of any materials you'll need to do the Bonus Activities.

6. Pray for each member of your group during the course of the week.

Enrichment

1. If you want a daily plan for reading through the Gospel of John during this unit, read the following sections this week:
   - Day 1: John 1:1-18
   - Day 2: John 1:19-28
   - Day 3: John 1:29-34
   - Day 4: John 1:35-51
   - Day 5: John 2:1-11
   - Day 6: John 2:12-25
   - Day 7: John 3:1-21

2. Visit www.textweek.com and explore links related to this week's focus verse.

3. Watch the movie *Sister Act* (Touchstone/Disney, 1992) and reflect upon how the nuns live out an incarnational ministry in their neighborhood. How does this ministry change people?

For Further Reading

Available from www.augsburgfortress.org/store:

Social-Science Commentary on the Gospel of John by Bruce J. Malina and Richard L. Rohrbaugh (Fortress Pres, 1998). Describes the values, conflicts, and traditions of the ancient world.

Incarnation by Alister E. McGrath (Fortress Press, 2005). Provides art, poetry, prayer, and reflection on the Word made flesh.

SESSION TWO

John 3:1-21

Leader Session Guide

Focus Statement

Jesus is God's gift of love to the world. Through him, we receive salvation and new birth, and we live in God's presence forever.

Key Verse

For God so loved the world that he gave his only Son, so that everyone who believes in him may not perish but may have eternal life. John 3:16

Focus Image

© Digital Vision Ltd. / SuperStock

How Is It Possible for Us to Be in Relationship with God?

Session Preparation

Before You Begin . . .

You'll spend time in this lesson on how Christ makes it possible for us to be in relationship with God, living out our baptismal calling. If you are baptized, locate your baptismal date by checking your baptismal certificate or contacting the congregation where your baptism occurred. What does it mean to you that God claims us as God's own in Baptism and gives us a new birth again and again each day? If you aren't baptized, consider talking with a pastor to learn more and schedule a time for baptism.

Session Instructions

1. Read this Session Guide completely and highlight or underline any portions you wish to emphasize with the group. Note any Bonus Activities you wish to do.

2. View the Session Prep Video.

3. If you plan to do any special activities, check to see what materials you'll need, if any.

4. Have extra Bibles on hand in case a member of the group forgets to bring one.

Session Overview

Nicodemus's visit with Jesus is a story that contains one of the most quoted verses from the Bible: John 3:16. Taking a look at John 3:1-21 from the perspective of the four contexts will help you get deeper into the background and possible meanings of the text. You and your group will certainly get to the heart of the session question: How is it possible for us to be in relationship with God?

LITERARY CONTEXT

For John, the condition of your relationship with God is based on whether or not you accept Jesus as the Incarnate Word of God. Jesus makes a direct relationship with God possible.

The session Scripture text includes one of the key **literary devices** used by the Gospel of John: misunderstanding. Throughout the Gospel, you will see people struggling with issues of belief and

Session 2: John 3:1-21   19

SESSION TWO

> **? Literary devices:**
> Language forms created and used by an author to get a point across to the reader in a distinctive way. Literary devices include metaphors, irony, and the use of long discourses.

unbelief. The literary device of misunderstanding on the part of a character offers Jesus an opportunity to talk more extensively about the question at hand. Often, misunderstanding is directly tied to the use of a word that can, in fact, have two meanings. This form of double wordplay happens in the session text, in which "born from above" can also mean "born again."

Your group will look at the responses of Nicodemus, who exhibits misunderstanding of Jesus' words. Encourage your group to watch for other examples of misunderstanding as they occur in John.

You'll also look at the character of Nicodemus, who only appears in the Bible three brief times in John's Gospel. While his status as a believer is not clearly stated, it does appear that he becomes, at the very least, a sympathizer of Jesus and his followers. You'll compare the three incidents (John 3:1-21; 7:45-52; 19:38-42) to examine this progression.

HISTORICAL CONTEXT

It's helpful to know something about the social structure of New Testament times, especially in regard to Nicodemus and his role as a Pharisee. John says that Nicodemus was a Pharisee and "leader of the Jews," so we assume that he was part of the Jewish Council, the Sanhedrin. The Pharisees have their roots in the Old Testament books of Ezra and Nehemiah. Both books supported extreme separatism in order to maintain Israel's existence after the return to the homeland following the Babylonian exile, which ended in 538 B.C.E. (2 Chronicles 36:22-23). The Pharisees believed in a physical resurrection and the existence of angels and demons. They viewed the entirety of Hebrew Scriptures as canon or "accepted" Scripture, unlike the Sadducees, another group of Jewish leaders, who accepted as canon only the first five books of what we know as the Old Testament. It is unclear how much control the Pharisees had after the fall of the temple in 70 C.E., but it is theorized that after the temple was destroyed there was another movement toward separatism and strict observance of the Jewish rules of cleanliness. This means John's Gospel was most likely written during a time of religious upheaval.

>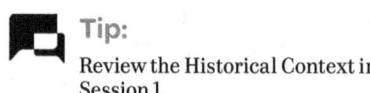
> **Tip:**
> Review the Historical Context in Session 1.

Your group will take a look at how John's Gospel describes the Pharisees in order to understand the political and social background of the time, and the challenges that Nicodemus may have faced.

SESSION TWO

LUTHERAN CONTEXT

In regards to the session Scripture text, you'll use the Lutheran approach to Scripture: What shows forth Christ? John 3:16 has often been described as the "gospel in miniature" because in one sentence it summarizes God's love for us as it is expressed through the death of God's Son. John 3:1-21 points to God's desire and intent to give us **eternal life,** the gift of dwelling forever in God's presence. It also defines Jesus' purpose in becoming the Incarnate Word who is sent by God to speak to us through his actions.

 Eternal life:
In the Gospel of John, this means dwelling in God's presence forever; it begins when one comes to believe that Jesus is God's Son, the Messiah.

You'll also look at the plain meaning of the text as you look at the reference in John 3:14 to Moses lifting up the serpent in the wilderness. Numbers 21:4-9 tells the story of the people rebelling against God. God then sends poisonous serpents to bite them. The people repent and ask Moses to pray to God to save them. God then provides the means for salvation by instructing Moses to lift a serpent on a pole so all will live. Likewise, Jesus will be "lifted up" on the cross to save the people of God from their sins.

DEVOTIONAL CONTEXT

One way to read Scripture devotionally is to place ourselves in the story. Group members will be invited to consider the similarities and differences between themselves and Nicodemus.

Today, readers of the Gospel of John find a strong connection between baptism and being born of "water and Spirit" (John 3:5). In the Small Catechism, Martin Luther speaks of the nature of the daily living out of one's baptism. When he speaks of the significance of baptism, he says, "It signifies that the old creature in us with all sins and evil desires is to be drowned and die through daily contrition and repentance, and on the other hand that daily a new person is to come forth and rise up to live before God in righteous and purity forever" (*The Book of Concord: the Confessions of the Evangelical Lutheran Church*, ed. Robert Kolb and Timothy J. Wengert, p. 360). Group members will explore what it means to live out baptismal callings each day.

Facilitator's Prayer

Dear Jesus, there are times when I can relate to Nicodemus's confusion all too well. I hear your words spoken in Scripture and through preaching, and I am sometimes perplexed about the meaning for me and my life. Open my heart and my ears to your Word, especially as I facilitate this group discussion. Keep me alert

SESSION TWO

to how those present are speaking your Word anew to me and to each other. And always help me relate your Word to my life. Amen.

Gather (10-15 minutes)

Check-in

Ask participants if they completed homework from last week that they'd like to share with the group as a review of last week's session. If there's no homework to share, give a brief recap of the session Scripture text and discussion. This will be especially helpful for any new members who may have joined the group this week.

Tip: Start the session with introductions again to incorporate newcomers. If you used name cards or tags during the last session, distribute them again. Encourage new members to make name cards or tags too.

Pray

Loving God, we thank you for bringing us together once again and ask for your presence in all of our thoughts and conversation. Open our ears and our hearts so that we might hear your Word spoken to us this day and understand its meaning for our lives. Empower each of us to live in celebration of the gifts of salvation, new birth, and life forever in God's presence. Amen.

Focus Activity

Tell about a wonderful gift you have received. What did you do with this gift? How did you respond to the giver?

Tip: Form pairs and offer them a few minutes to discuss. Then have everyone return to the large group and share some reflections. Ask the group to keep these conversations in mind during this session.

Open Scripture (10-15 minutes)

Read John 3:1-21.

- What phrase or image did you immediately connect with as this text was read?
- What confused you?
- What did you find comforting?

Here are options to introduce the text:

Place a small bowl of water and a cross in the center of the table or at some other focal point. Ask the group to look at these as the text is read. At the conclusion, invite learners to dip their fingers in the water and make the sign of the cross on their foreheads in remembrance of baptism.

Tip: Solicit volunteer readers in advance as you work through the sessions. Keep in mind that some people are uncomfortable reading aloud.

SESSION TWO

Play music softly in the background as one or two group members read the text. Try to find music that fits the tone of the passage—perhaps something meditative.

Join the Conversation (25-55 minutes)

Literary Context

1. The phrase "kingdom of God" appears many times in Matthew, Mark, and Luke, but only twice in John's Gospel (John 3:3 and 3:5). John uses the phrase "eternal life" instead to define our relationship with God. The session Scripture text points to God's desire and intent to give us eternal life, the gift of dwelling forever in God's presence. It also defines God's purpose in sending Jesus, the Incarnate Word.

- Scan John 3:1-21 and count the number of times "kingdom of God" and "eternal life" appear. Why do you suppose John is so focused on our relationship with God?
- Write down key words from the text that tell about God's purpose in sending Jesus.

Bonus Activity:

Read John 4:7-26, about Jesus' encounter with a Samaritan woman. How are misunderstanding and wordplay used in this text? What is the result of Jesus' encounter with the Samaritan woman? What are the similarities and differences between Jesus' encounter with the Samaritan woman and with Nicodemus?

Bonus Activity:

Discuss Jesus' encounter with the Samaritan woman (John 4:7-26). Have two volunteers role-play this meeting, based on the group discussion.

2. John 3:1-21 and other texts in this Gospel focus on our relationship to Jesus and to God through belief or unbelief. As characters like Nicodemus struggle with these things, Jesus takes the opportunity to explain the deeper meaning of things that are heavenly. The misunderstanding of the characters can be viewed as a literary device, a language form created and used by an author to get a point across to the reader in a distinctive way. This literary device is also used in another way—as wordplay through the use of words that can, in fact, have two meanings. For example, in John 3:1-21, the Greek word *anothen*, which means "born from above," can also mean "born again." Here Jesus is not speaking of a literal "rebirth," but of a spiritual rebirth.

- Where do you see misunderstanding and wordplay at work in John 3:1-21?
- Role-play the meeting between Jesus and Nicodemus.
- What is the result of Jesus' encounter with Nicodemus?

Tip:

Have the group discuss the meeting between Jesus and Nicodemus. Then invite two volunteers to do the role-play, based on the group discussion.

Tip:

Have two volunteers read the Scripture passages aloud. Encourage other group members to follow along in their Bibles and make notes if they wish.

3. The character Nicodemus appears only in the Gospel of John and then only three times. John 3:1-21 doesn't show us Nicodemus's response to Jesus. Read John 7:45-52 and 19:38-42 to find out more about this man.

Session 2: John 3:1-21

SESSION TWO

- How would you describe Nicodemus after reading these additional passages?
- If you were the casting director for a play, who would you choose as actor for the role of Nicodemus?

Historical Context

1. As a leader of the Jews, Nicodemus may have been part of the decision-making Jewish Council, or Sanhedrin. As a Pharisee, Nicodemus belonged to a group with roots in the Old Testament books of Ezra and Nehemiah. (These books supported keeping the people of Israel separate, in order to maintain their existence, after they returned to their homeland following an exile in Babylonia.) In Jesus' day, Pharisees were educated, faithful leaders dedicated to teaching the Jewish Scriptures and applying the law to everyday living. They believed in a physical resurrection, the existence of angels and demons, and in viewing all of Hebrew Scriptures as "canon" or accepted Scripture.

Bonus Activity:
Water is a key image in Jesus' meeting with Nicodemus (and with the Samaritan woman). It gives life and brings new life. Create pairs or trios and give each a piece of paper to create a "living water" collage. Have magazines, glue, and scissors on hand. Should they wish to, participants can also draw their interpretation of "living water."

Read the following passages and describe the relationship between the Pharisees and Jesus in John's Gospel.

- John 1:24-25; 4:1-3; 7:31-32, 45-52
- John 8:12-20; 9:13-41; 11:45-57
- John 12:17-19, 42-43; 18:1-3

Tip:
Form three groups and assign each group one of the three sets of texts listed here. Have everyone return to the large group to share the results of their reading and group discussion.

2. How risky do you think it was for Nicodemus, a Pharisee, to seek out Jesus and talk to him? Plot your answer on the line below and explain your response.

Not at all risky ◆----------------------------------◆ Very risky

Lutheran Context

1. Martin Luther called the Bible the manger that holds the Christ child. He looked at passages in the Old and New Testaments and asked, "What shows forth Christ?" We can use this approach to look at John 3:1-21.

Tip:
The Pharisees have often been portrayed simply as Jesus' opponents. Encourage learners to dig into the texts to discover how John's Gospel in particular portrays this group.

- What does this text reveal to us about Christ?
- What does this text reveal to us about God?
- How does this text draw us or invite us into a relationship with Christ?
- Some say John 3:16 is the "gospel in miniature." Do you agree with this? Why or why not?

Bonus Activity:
Read Leviticus 20:22-26. What does this say about the proper observance of laws?

2. Another Lutheran approach to the Bible is called "the plain meaning of the text," which looks at what the obvious meaning

Bonus Activity:
Read 2 Chronicles 36:1-23 and use chart paper or a whiteboard to list key findings about the Babylonian Exile.

Bonus Activity:
Read Nehemiah 1:1-11; 9:1-37. Why might the people want to become separatists after their return to Jerusalem following the time of exile in Babylonia? How might this help them?

24 John Leader Guide

of the text would have been to the original audience. The original readers and hearers of the Gospel of John would have been very familiar with the story of Moses lifting up a serpent on a pole, which is referred to in John 3:14. To get at the plain meaning of the text, then, read this story in Numbers 21:4-9.

- Does the story in Numbers 21:4-9 help you understand John 3:1-21? Why or why not?
- If a friend asked you, "Why did God send Jesus into the world?" what would you say?

Devotional Context

1. The Gospel of John doesn't provide many details about Nicodemus, but it does tell us that he talked with Jesus, asked questions, and, in the end, helped with Jesus' burial.

- What similarities or differences do you see between yourself and Nicodemus?
- What questions would you ask Jesus?
- What risks would you take for Jesus' sake?

2. Look back at the Focus Image at the start of this session. We are reborn in Baptism and live in Christ's love and God's presence forever.

- List some ways to remember these promises at the start of each day.
- How can you celebrate the gift of God's love in Christ?

3. Consider the Scripture texts you have studied and the conversation you have had in this session.

- How is it possible for us to be in relationship with God?
- How do you respond to the amazing love of God demonstrated in Christ?

Wrap-up

1. Remind learners of the Focus Activity. How does God's gift of Jesus Christ compare with other gifts?

2. Point out any "ah-ha" moments that you noticed in the session. Ask: What "ah-ha" moments did you experience?

3. Ask if there are any questions learners wanted to explore further, but didn't have time for. Write these questions on chart paper. Solicit volunteers to do further research to share with the group.

Tip:
The story in Numbers 21:4-9 takes place after Moses led the people of Israel out of Egypt, where they had been slaves.

Tip:
List responses to the questions on chart paper or a whiteboard.

Bonus Activity:
Hand out paper and a variety of markers, pastels, etc. for use in this activity. Have some clay available, too, in case someone wants to go "3-D." Instruct learners to create a drawing, illustration, or clay model of the meaning of John 3:1-21 for them. Share these in the larger group. This can also be done as homework and shared at the next session.

Bonus Activity:
Play, sing, or read *Evangelical Lutheran Worship* hymn 660, "Lift High the Cross." Reflect upon its meaning in light of your discussion of John 3:1-21.

SESSION TWO

Tip:
Encourage those who are baptized to celebrate their baptismal anniversaries each year.

Bonus Activity:
Solicit volunteers to role-play a discussion between someone who sees baptism as a one-day event and another who sees it as being a daily calling.

4. Ask group members if they would like to do any of the homework activities listed in the Extending the Conversation section. Don't pressure anyone into participating, but ask those who would like to do further work to share their findings at the start of the next session.

Pray

O God, we thank you for the gift of your Son, Jesus, who came to show us the extreme depth of your love for us through his death on the cross. We also give thanks for the new birth we receive in baptism through water and the Spirit. Help us to live out our baptism each day, celebrating the relationship we have with you through Christ. We pray in the name of Jesus, our Lord and Savior. Amen.

Extending the Conversation (5 minutes)

Homework

1. Read the Scripture text for the next session: John 6:25-59. If time permits, read all of John 3:22—6:59 (see below for a daily reading plan).

2. Reread John 3:1-21 and consider the themes that touch you the most. Write a prayer or poem based on one of those themes.

3. Create a diorama (a three-dimensional scene) or write a script that dramatizes your interpretation of Jesus' encounter with Nicodemus. What will you be sure to include?

4. If you are baptized, research your baptismal date and the location. Interview anyone who was present that day. Write down what you learn in a journal or scrapbook and add photos, if available. If you are not baptized, talk to a pastor to learn more or schedule a baptism.

SESSION TWO

Looking Ahead

1. Read the Scripture text for the next session: John 6:25-59.

2. Read through the Leader Guide for the next session and mark portions you wish to highlight for the group.

3. Make a checklist of any materials you'll need to do the Bonus Activities.

4. Continue to pray for members of your group during the week.

Enrichment

1. If you want a daily plan for reading through the Gospel of John during this unit, read the following sections this week:
    Day 1: John 3:22-36
    Day 2: John 4:1-45
    Day 3: John 4:46—5:18
    Day 4: John 5:19-47
    Day 5: John 6:1-15
    Day 6: John 6:16-24
    Day 7: John 6:25-59

2. Use a concordance or online Bible search engine to look up other New Testament passages related to water and Spirit. Note any patterns or commonalities you discover.

3. Go to www.textweek.com and follow some of the links related to this session's Scripture text. What do you find?

For Further Reading

Peoples of the New Testament World: An Illustrated Guide by William A. Simmons (Hendrickson Publishers, 2008). Analyzes the major groups of people that existed in New Testament times.

Available from www.augsburgfortress.org/store:

Baptism: A User's Guide by Martin Marty (Augsburg Books, 2008). Describes how Baptism is at the heart of the everyday, lifelong spiritual journey.

From Jesus to the Gospels: Interpreting the New Testament in Its Context by Helmut Koester (Fortress Press, 2007). Offers insights into the message of Jesus and the factors that shaped the Gospels and other early Christian literature.

New Proclamation Commentary on the Gospels, ed. Andrew Gregory (Fortress Press, 2006). Provides commentary on the four Gospels and highlights important themes.

SESSION THREE

John 6:25-59

Leader Session Guide

Focus Statement
When we share the "bread of life" in the Eucharist, we share in Jesus' life, death, and resurrection.

Key Verse
I am the living bread that came down from heaven. Whoever eats of this bread will live forever; and the bread that I will give for the life of the world is my flesh.
John 6:51

Focus Image

© Nora Scarlett / SuperStock

What Does It Mean that Jesus Is the "Bread of Life"?

Session Preparation

Before You Begin . . .

Reflect upon how you experience Jesus as the "bread of life." How is your faith life fed and nurtured at the communion table? What does Holy Communion mean for your life and daily living? How do you experience Jesus' real presence at Holy Communion? Journal your thoughts.

Session Instructions

1. View the Session Prep Video.

2. Read this Session Guide completely and highlight or underline any portions you wish to emphasize with the group. Note any Bonus Activities you wish to do.

3. If you plan to do any special activities, check to see what materials you'll need, if any.

4. Have extra Bibles on hand in case a member of the group forgets to bring one.

Session Overview

The Gospel of John is the only Gospel that does not tell the story of Jesus' institution of the sacrament of Holy Communion. However, the session Scripture text is rich in **eucharistic** imagery. The central questions that your group will focus on will be: What does it mean that Jesus is the bread of life? What does that mean for us today?

LITERARY CONTEXT

The writer of the Gospel of John utilizes some distinctive literary devices not used by the Synoptic Gospels of Matthew, Mark, and Luke. The last session examined the use of wordplay and misunderstanding. This session will give your group the opportunity to look at the first use of John's "I am" sayings. These sayings are metaphors or descriptive word pictures that give us additional information about who Jesus really is. Just as using the words "I am" offer each of us the chance to more clearly state who we are, these same words offer John's central character, Jesus, the chance to reveal further details about his identity and purpose and what this means for his disciples.

SESSION THREE

 **Eucharistic:**
Related to Holy Communion. *Eucharist* means "thanksgiving" in Greek.

You'll look at other "I am" sayings to see what images John uses in his Gospel. These include light of the world (John 8:12 and 9:5), gate for the sheep (10:7, 9), good shepherd (10:11, 14), resurrection and the life (11:25-26), the way, the truth, and the life (14:6), and true vine (15:1, 5).

In John 6:35, Jesus says, "I am the bread of life." Your group will explore the metaphor of "bread of life" and its meaning for the early Christian community and for us.

Historical Context

Bread was a staple in a person's diet in biblical times, an essential part of everyday life. For the original hearers and readers of John's Gospel, saying Jesus is the bread of life meant that Jesus was essential to daily living.

From a sociological standpoint, a person's origins indicated rank and status. In John 6:38, Jesus states that he has "come down from heaven." The community that the Gospel of John emerged from would have understood that if Jesus came down from heaven, it was natural that he could return there. This is another theme carried throughout the book of John, particularly at his glorification on the cross.

Judaism prohibited adherents from eating anything containing blood, since blood was literally interpreted as the source of life itself. (See: Genesis 9:4; Leviticus 17:11; and Deuteronomy 12:23.) Therefore, Jesus' claim in John 6:54 that it is necessary to eat his flesh and drink his blood would have horrified those with these traditional Jewish beliefs.

Yet, John uses the strong metaphorical language of eating Jesus' flesh and blood when he speaks of the Eucharist. Those with little knowledge of the Lord's Supper would have misinterpreted the meaning of these words, thinking them horrifying and possibly cannibalistic. (See 1 Corinthians 11:23-26; Matthew 26:26-29; Mark 14:22-25; and Luke 22:14-20.)

Your group will look at the historical background of this text to understand why early Christians were sometimes thought to be cannibalistic. The text also reminds us that the Christian community of John's day had already established an "in-house" language that was shocking to those outside the community who did not know or understand its faith practices.

SESSION THREE

LUTHERAN CONTEXT

You'll use the Lutheran interpretive principle of Scripture interprets Scripture to take you deeper into today's text. In John 6:31-32, you'll find Jesus' reference to manna coming down from heaven. He later describes himself as the bread that has come down from heaven. In Exodus 16:1-35 you'll explore the similarities and differences between the manna given by God to Moses and the Israelites in the wilderness and Jesus, the bread of life. While those who ate the manna in the wilderness eventually died, those who partake of Jesus' body and blood are given the gift of eternal life.

You'll also look at the Lutheran belief in the *real presence* of Jesus in Holy Communion. This is the belief that Christ is fully present in, with, and under the bread and wine. Martin Luther wrote that the Sacrament of the Altar is "the true body and blood of our Lord Jesus Christ under the bread and wine, instituted by Christ himself for us Christians to eat and to drink" (Small Catechism, p. 33).

DEVOTIONAL CONTEXT

In the previous session, you talked about the strong connection between baptism and John 3:5. This session points to a strong connection between Jesus' bread of life discourse and the Eucharist. In John 6:52-58, Jesus describes the benefits of eating his body and blood. These benefits include life both now and in the future, an intimate union with Jesus now and for all time, and being raised by Jesus on "the last day."

In the Large Catechism, Martin Luther says that "the Lord's Supper is given as a daily food and sustenance so that our faith may be refreshed and strengthened and that it may not succumb in the struggle but become stronger and stronger. For the new life should be one that continually develops and progresses" (*Book of Concord*, 469:24-25).

Your group will explore the meaning of celebrating Holy Communion. How are we strengthened and nourished for daily life at the Lord's Supper? How does sharing in the Lord's body and blood empower each individual to grow in his or her faith?

Facilitator's Prayer

O Jesus, bread of life, through you our lives and our faith are fed and nourished. May I never forget that through your gift of Holy Communion I share in your life, death, and resurrection and receive

SESSION THREE

the gifts of forgiveness and the promise of eternal life. Bless our Bible study session with insight and inspiration as we explore your real presence in our lives. Empower me to be compassionate in my leadership and listening and so that I, too, might grow from our time together. Amen.

Gather (10-15 minutes)

Check-in

Tip: Remember to include introductions if there are new members joining the group. Use the name cards or tags from the previous two sessions to help people remember names.

Ask learners if they want to share any homework completed from the last session or any further insights. If no one chooses to share, give a brief recap of the previous session.

Pray

Tip: As people enter the room, ask them to briefly list any joys or concerns on chart paper for inclusion in the prayers. Cue one or two volunteers to read these at the given time.

Offer this prayer for the group:

We give you thanks, O God, that your Son, Jesus, is indeed the bread of life from heaven who feeds and nourishes us regularly through our participation in Holy Communion. During our time together in Bible study, open our hearts and ears to new understandings of what Holy Communion means for our daily living.

As we come together, we also pray for joys and concerns and for those who are in our hearts and on our minds. Especially we pray for . . .

In Jesus' name we pray. Amen.

Focus Activity

Reflect on the Focus Image. What does hunger feel like? Compare physical hunger and spiritual hunger.

Open Scripture (10-15 minutes)

Tip: Have learners form pairs for discussion and return to the large group to share thoughts and reflections.

Read John 6:25-59.

- What image did you most connect with?
- How did you feel as you heard the text?
- What do you want to know more about?

Here are options to introduce the text:

32   John Leader Guide

SESSION THREE

Place a loaf of bread and a chalice of wine in the center of the table and ask participants to focus on these items as the text is read.

Set up a series of illustrations and photos related to this text (www.textweek.com or an online image search are good starting points). Display these images around the room, and invite learners to walk through the "gallery" as you slowly read the Bible passage two or three times.

Join the Conversation (25-55 minutes)

Literary Context

1. In the session 2 Scripture text, the writer of the Gospel of John used the literary device of misunderstanding. Nicodemus's misunderstandings gave Jesus opportunities to say more about the questions at hand. Another literary device is at work in the Scripture text for this session: the "I am" sayings. These sayings, listed in the chart below, are not found in any other Gospel. They make up a very distinctive literary device that the author uses to more clearly define who Jesus is and what this means for his disciples.

The "I AM" Sayings of Jesus in John's Gospel

Two Kinds of "I AM" sayings appear in the Gospel of John.

Absolute "I AM" Sayings	"I AM" Sayings with a Descriptive Image
4:26 "I am he, the one who is speaking to you."	6:35 "I am the bread of life."
6:20 "It is I; do not be afraid."	6:51 "I am the living bread that came down from heaven."
8:24 "I told you that you would die in your sins, for you will die in your sins unless you believe that I am he."	8:12 "I am the light of the world."
8:28 "When you have lifted up the Son of Man, then you will realize that I am he, and that I do nothing on my own, but I speak these things as the Father instructed me."	9:5 "I am the light of the world."
8:58 "Very truly, I tell you, before Abraham was, I am."	10:7 "I am the gate for the sheep."
13:19 "I tell you this now, before it occurs, so that when it does occur, you may believe that I am he."	10:9 "I am the gate."
18:5, 8 "I am he."	10:11, 14 "I am the good shepherd."
	11:25-26 "I am the resurrection and the life."
	14:6 "I am the way, and the truth, and the life."
	15:1 "I am the true vine."
	15:5 "I am the vine, you are the branches."

Copyright © 2009 Augsburg Fortress

SESSION THREE

 Bonus Activity:
Give each pair or trio a piece of paper and some colored markers and have them write 21st-century "I am" sayings that are particularly relevant for contemporary Christians and our relationship with Jesus. Then discuss: How did you decide what to include in this list?

 Tip:
For the comfort of less outspoken participants, consider breaking into pairs or trios to discuss this question.

- How well do you think these sayings tell who Jesus is and what this means for his followers? Plot an X at the spot on the continuum below that best reflects your thoughts on this question.

Not well at all ◄------------------------------------► Very well

- John's Gospel does not include a story in which Jesus institutes Holy Communion (also called the Sacrament of the Altar, the Lord's Supper, and the Eucharist—from the Greek word for "thanksgiving"). However, the session Scripture text, which can be described as a discourse or speech on the bread of life, is rich in eucharistic images. Read John 6:25-59 and list what is said about the bread of life or bread from heaven. How is this bread different from other bread?

2. Jesus points out that the disciples were looking for him only because they "ate [their] fill of the loaves" (John 6:26). This relates to an earlier story in John 6, the feeding of the five thousand.

 Bonus Activity:
Play a recording of "I Am the Bread of Life" (*ELW* 485). Play it a second time and invite the group to sing along. Discuss thoughts or feelings the hymn provoked as participants heard it and sang it. Break into trios and have each small group write a poem or hymn verse based on the session Scripture text. What did they include and why?

- Read John 6:1-14. What connections do you see between this story and John 6:25-59? What connections do you see between this story and Jesus' proclamation that he is the "bread of life"?

Historical Context

1. Bread was a staple in a person's diet in biblical times, an essential part of everyday life.

- What would "I am the bread of life" have meant to the original hearers and readers?

 Tip:
Have a collection of commentaries and Bible dictionaries on hand to aid your discussion.

2. In biblical times, where people came from directly impacted their status in society: "One could not aspire to ascend to the sky (assume divine honor status) unless one was originally from that region. Attempting to do so was the sin of the King of Babylon (Isaiah 14:12-14), whose arrogance was severely punished" (*Social Science Commentary on the Gospel of John* by Bruce Malina and Richard Rohrbaugh, p. 85).

 Bonus Activity:
Break into trios. Briefly list what Jesus says about his origins in these passages: John 7:28-29; 8:23; 8:42; 13:3-4; 16:27-28; and 17:8. Have everyone reconvene in the larger group to share findings. What is the Gospel of John saying about Jesus in these passages?

- Compile a list of the verses in John 6:25-59 in which Jesus talks about his origin.
- What do these verses say about who Jesus is?
- What is the reaction of the Jewish religious leaders?

3. Jewish faith prohibited the eating of anything containing blood. Imagine, then, the reaction of faithful Jews to the claim that it is necessary to eat Jesus' flesh and drink his blood (John 6:52-57).

34   John Leader Guide

- Read Genesis 9:4; Leviticus 17:11; and Deuteronomy 12:23 and list what these laws say about eating blood.
- Why do you suppose Jesus' reference to eating his flesh and drinking his blood might have been disturbing to some people?

Lutheran Context

1. Let's use the Lutheran principle of "Scripture interprets Scripture" to look at this session's text in light of another. In John 6:31-32, Jesus refers to the Israelites eating manna, bread from heaven, which was supplied by God during the people's 40-year trek in the wilderness. Read Exodus 16:1-35, which tells about the manna God sent after the people complained to Moses and Aaron that they were hungry.

- What themes are present in both Exodus 16:1-35 and John 6:25-59?
- What are the differences between the texts?
- What does it mean that Jesus is the bread that came down from heaven?

2. Lutherans have traditionally believed in the *real presence* of Jesus in Holy Communion. This is the belief that Christ is fully present in, with, and under the bread and wine. Martin Luther wrote that the Sacrament of the Altar is "the true body and blood of our Lord Jesus Christ under the bread and wine, instituted by Christ himself for us Christians to eat and to drink" (*Luther's Small Catechism with Evangelical Lutheran Worship Texts*, Augsburg Fortress, 2008, p. 33).

- How does John 6:25-59 support the real presence of Christ in Holy Communion?

Devotional Context

- Read John 6:52-58. What benefits do we receive from eating Jesus' flesh and drinking his blood?
- Reflect upon this session's discussion and your experiences of receiving Holy Communion. How does the Lord's Supper feed and nourish you for daily living?
- Tell about a time when the Eucharist was particularly meaningful to you.
- What term do you prefer: Holy Communion, the Sacrament of the Altar, the Lord's Supper, the Eucharist, or something else? Why?
- Create a "Bread of Life" collage that depicts what it means to you when Jesus says, "I am the bread of life."

Tip:
These texts are brief, so consider asking for volunteers or read them yourself.

Bonus Activity:
Break into small groups and discuss how and why early Christians were sometimes thought to be cannibalistic. Then ask for volunteers to role-play a conversation between an early Christian trying to explain the meaning of Holy Communion to someone not part of the early Christian movement.

Bonus Activity:
Distribute copies of Martin Luther's Small Catechism. Instruct learners to turn to the section on the Sacrament of the Altar, pp. 33–35. Enlist one or two volunteers to read it aloud. What are the most important points Luther makes about the sacrament? How does this relate to John 6:25-59? Ask learners to journal their thoughts.

Tip:
If possible, give each learner a copy of *Luther's Small Catechism with Evangelical Lutheran Worship Texts* (Augsburg Fortress, 2008) to keep. Another option is to distribute *Evangelical Lutheran Worship* and turn to page 1166.

Bonus Activity:
Explore law and gospel in the session Scripture text. Form two groups and give each one a piece of chart paper and markers. Assign one group the task of looking for the law, or demands, in John 6:25-59. Assign the other group the task of looking for the gospel, or promises of God, in the text. (Law places demands upon us while grace, or gospel, is that which speaks the message of God's love and forgiveness for us.) Instruct the two groups to list their findings to share with the entire group.

Tip:
Distribute poster paper, markers, magazines, scissors, and glue. Encourage participants to have fun and be creative.

SESSION THREE

Bonus Activity:

Ecce Panis Angerlorum (Behold the Bread of Angels) is a part of a Gregorian chant written by Thomas Aquinas. Locate a CD or MP3 recording and play it for the group. Ask learners to meditate on the meaning of John 6:25-59 while they are listening. Ask what feelings the music elicits in them. Encourage each learner to journal or draw a picture while listening to the recording.

Tip:

Various translations of *Ecce Panis Angelorum* can be located by typing the title into an Internet search engine.

Tip:

Consider visiting www.bookoffaith.org/bof_new/related_resources.aspx to do research on questions that the group still has.

Wrap-up

1. Return to the the Focus Activity about physical hunger and spiritual hunger. What new thoughts do learners have about this?

2. Point out any "ah-ha" moments that you noticed in the session. What "ah-ha" moments did learners experience?

3. List any new questions that learners now have. Solicit volunteers to do further research to share with the group.

4. Ask group members if they felt particularly challenged or confused by anything in today's session.

Pray

We give you thanks, O God, for this time we have spent together exploring what it means that your Son, Jesus, is the bread of life who came down from heaven. We also thank you for nourishing our faith and giving us forgiveness and eternal life through the precious gift of Holy Communion. Open our hearts each time we share in the Eucharist to feel Jesus' presence and power in our lives, so that we are continually strengthened and renewed for daily living. Thank you for the witness of the early church shared through the writers of the New Testament texts—especially through the Gospel of John. Amen.

Extending the Conversation (5 minutes)

Homework

1. Read the Scripture text for the next session: John 9:1-41. If time permits, read all of John 6:60—9:41 (see below for a daily reading plan).

2. Interview several people, young and old, and ask them why Holy Communion is important to them in their faith journey. Ask if you can share their responses with this group.

3. Journal any reflections that you've had as a result of this session. Consider sharing these with the group at the next session.

SESSION THREE

Looking Ahead

1. Reflect on how things went during this session. What did you learn about facilitating a Bible study? What worked well? What might you have done differently?

2. Reflect upon the preferred learning styles of your adult learners. What came easier to your group? Do they prefer learning through visual means, conversational means, or through physical activities?

3. Read the Scripture text for the next session: John 9:1-41.

4. Read through the Leader Guide for the next session and mark the portions you wish to highlight for the group.

5. Make a checklist of any materials you'll need to do the Bonus Activities.

6. Continue to pray for members of your group during the week.

Enrichment

1. If you want a daily plan for reading through the Gospel of John during this unit, read the following sections this week:
    Day 1: John 6:60-71
    Day 2: John 7:1-52
    Day 3: John 8:1-11
    Day 4: John 8:12-38
    Day 5: John 8:39-59
    Day 6: John 9:1-12
    Day 7: John 9:13-41

2. Watch the YouTube video "Jesus, the Bread of Life" (www.youtube.com/watch?v=o2gQawQ7F0A). Record your thoughts and impressions in a journal.

3. Conduct an Internet search on what it means when John refers to Jesus as the "Son of Man." Compare John's use of the title "Son of Man" with how it is used in Matthew, Mark, and Luke.

SESSION THREE

For Further Reading

Available from www.augsburgfortress.org/store:

The Book of Concord: the Confessions of the Evangelical Lutheran Church, ed. Robert Kolb and Timothy J. Wengert (Fortress Press, 2000). Provides foundational texts of Lutheran identity and theology.

Daily Bread, Holy Meal: Opening the Gifts of Holy Communion by Samuel Torvend (Augsburg Fortress, 2004). Describes the gifts of Holy Communion and discusses the significance of eating and drinking with Jesus of Nazareth in a world of great need.

From Symposium to Eucharist: The Banquet in the Early Christian World by Dennis E. Smith (Fortress Press, 2003). Describes the important place banquets held in creating community, sharing values, and connecting with the divine.

Symbolism in the Fourth Gospel: Meaning, Mystery, Community, 2nd ed., by Craig Koester (Fortress Press). Uses the symbolic language of the Gospel of John to explore its texts.

SESSION FOUR

John 9:1-41

Leader Session Guide

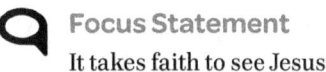
Focus Statement
It takes faith to see Jesus.

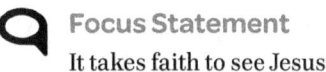
Key Verse
Jesus said, "I came into this world for judgment so that those who do not see may see, and those who do see may become blind." John 9:39

Focus Image

© fStop / SuperStock

Who Can See Jesus?

Session Preparation

Before You Begin . . .

Take some time to reflect upon your own definitions of sin and judgment. Have you ever thought that an illness or disability was the direct result of sin? Has anyone ever claimed that an illness you suffered from was the result of your sin? If so, how did that feel? Reflect on these experiences as you facilitate this session on Jesus' reinterpreting and redefining the meaning of sin and judgment.

Session Instructions

1. View the Session Prep Video.

2. Read this Session Guide completely and highlight or underline any portions you wish to emphasize with the group. Note any Bonus Activities you wish to do.

3. If you plan to do any special activities, check to see what materials you'll need, if any.

4. Have extra Bibles on hand in case a member of the group forgets to bring one.

Session Overview

HISTORICAL CONTEXT

Many biblical scholars believe the tension and conflict between John's community and the Jewish religious leaders is an underlying theme for this Gospel. The Jewish Christians may have been cast out of the synagogue around 90 C.E. If this was the case, the people in John's community would have been considered social outcasts by the Jewish religious leaders. John's community may have been an **"antisociety"** because it was considered socially unacceptable (*Social Science Commentary on the Gospel of John*). Your group will reflect upon the historical background of this story and why John might have thought it necessary to write a Gospel that spoke to the specific needs of his outcast community.

Because most of us are unfamiliar with the health care culture of Jesus' day, you'll also reflect upon Jesus' healing and performance of signs in light of the sociological system of New Testament times. While professional physicians did practice, they were not usually available to ordinary peasants and townspeople. The majority of

SESSION FOUR

Antisociety:
A group that goes against the established norms of acceptable society.

the population relied upon either the popular sector, comprised of family and the immediate community, or folk healers who had an established reputation of being able to restore health to sick individuals. Jesus would have been considered a folk healer by the people of his day. Knowing this can shed a different light on this text and also on the intense questioning of the former blind man by the Pharisees. Your group will look at this miracle story from this interesting sociological perspective.

LITERARY CONTEXT

The story of the healing of the blind man is dramatically told. It's full of action and intense interplay between the Pharisees and the characters they interrogate about this miracle—first, the former blind man, then his parents, and then the man again. As this drama unfolds, we can see how the miracle of the man's healing gradually elicits faith in him. Yet throughout the story, the Pharisees are blind to Jesus' true identity and are shown to be lacking in faith. Your group will look at the **rising action** and interpersonal interplay in this story and how they contribute to the story's climax.

Rising action:
The increase in action in a story's plot, especially as it approaches the climax.

During biblical times it was commonly believed that there was a connection between sin and illness. This is why the disciples question Jesus in John 9:3, asking if it was the sins of the man or of his parents that caused his blindness. Jesus responds that there is no connection between a sin and the man's disability. This story shows that through Jesus, "sin" is reinterpreted to mean not accepting God's presence through Jesus, God's Son. And, how a person is judged depends on his or her acceptance of Jesus. This literary tool of giving words a new meaning through the person of Jesus is common throughout the Gospel of John.

LUTHERAN CONTEXT

The Lutheran principle of Scripture interprets Scripture will give your group another opportunity to look at how the theological concepts of sin and judgment are redefined in the Gospel of John. You'll look at and reflect upon passages from John 3:19-21; 5:22-30; and 16:8-11, in which Jesus speaks more about the meaning of judgment. In John 3:19-21, Jesus says he has been sent into the world to bring light to the people's darkness and unbelief. In John 5:22-30, it is clear that through belief, one attains eternal life (a deep connection with God through the Son) now and for all time. And the correlation is drawn that if the Son is not honored, the Father is not honored. Finally, John 16:8-11 speaks of the coming of the Holy Spirit, or Advocate, who will further redefine judgment and show the world that its understanding of judgment is wrong.

Lutherans speak of the **dialectic** of law and gospel, contending that both are necessary in biblical interpretation. The law shows us our sins, makes demands, and places expectations upon us. The gospel offers us good news and speaks God's forgiveness and promise to us. You'll examine the session Scripture text using the lenses of both law and gospel to gain a deeper understanding of the meaning from a Lutheran perspective.

Devotional Context

While Jesus heals the man of his physical blindness, this story in the Gospel of John explores the nature of spiritual blindness. The man, though once blind, comes to a gradual recognition of Jesus as the one sent by God to both save and judge the world. However, it is clear as the drama unfolds that the Pharisees and religious leaders neither recognize where Jesus has come from nor who he is. Because they do not have the former blind man's eyes of faith, John's Gospel defines them as "spiritually blind."

Your group will examine what it means to be spiritually blind. You'll reflect upon how it feels to look at life and its events through the eyes of faith and what it might feel like to interpret those same events from a non-spiritual perspective, or perhaps with eyes tightly closed.

As you talk about "blindness," be aware that this may be a highly sensitive area for some with visual impairments. Be inclusive and open to them and their unique perspective in interpreting this text.

Facilitator's Prayer

O Jesus, healer and giver of insight, I know that at times my eyes are closed to your presence in my life. Sometimes I'm too frazzled and busy to notice. At other times my eyes are too tightly closed to see and honor your presence through those people whose lives touch mine in significant and loving ways. I pray that you will open my eyes to your presence in our session. As I facilitate this session, empower me to invite others to see you, too. Amen.

Dialectic:
A method of argumentation that identifies opposing thoughts or views in order to more clearly define each one.

SESSION FOUR

Tip:
If there are new members in the group, have participants form pairs and take turns introducing each other by saying one memorable thing about the other person.

Gather (10-15 minutes)

Check-in

Ask learners if they want to share any homework completed from the last session or any further insights. If no one chooses to share, give a brief recap of the previous session.

Pray

Offer a time of silent prayer and reflection. Ask learners to think of the people they know with spiritual and physical needs. After a few minutes of silence, pray:

Gracious and holy God, give us diligence to seek you, wisdom to perceive you, and patience to wait for you. Grant us, O God, a mind to meditate on you; eyes to behold you; ears to listen for your word; a heart to love you; and a life to proclaim you; through the power of the Spirit of Jesus Christ, our Savior and Lord. Amen. (ELW, p. 76)

Focus Activity

Look at the Focus Image. How would you describe this picture? Tell about a time when fog kept you from seeing something, or made it difficult for you to find your way.

Open Scripture (10-15 minutes)

Have one person read the text as participants close their eyes and imagine they are present in the action.

Tip:
Using multiple readers can highlight the drama of the session Scripture text. Give them an opportunity to do a practice run before they read the text in the session.

Choose various readers to take the part of narrators and characters in the text. Have characters read the dialogue.

Read John 9:1-41.

1. What did you find striking?

2. What image or scene stands out?

3. What do you wonder about?

Join the Conversation (25-55 minutes)

Historical Context

1. Many scholars believe that John's Jewish Christian community was in an intense conflict with the religious leaders of the

SESSION FOUR

synagogue. The Jewish Christians may actually have been cast out of the synagogue around 90 C.E. (see John 9:22). Becoming outcasts, cut off from their Jewish roots, would have thrust the people of this community into an identity crisis.

- Look at John 9:1-41 again. What might this story say to people who had been cut off from their roots?
- What new insights do you have when you look at the story from this perspective?

2. Health care in Jesus' day was very different from today. Ordinary people did not have access to the professional physicians of the day. Instead they primarily relied upon their family and community during illness or on folk healers—individuals with a reputation for being able to restore people to health. Jesus would have been considered a folk healer by the people of his day.

- Review John 9:8-12. Is this how you would expect ordinary townspeople of Jesus' day to respond to the healing of the blind man? Why or why not?
- Imagine yourself watching the Pharisees interrogate the blind man and his parents. Why do they need to investigate whether the man was really born blind? What do they conclude?

Literary Context

1. Screenplay writers and playwrights use the term "rising action" to talk about the increase of action in a plot, especially as it approaches the story's climax.

- What is the climax of the story of the healing of the blind man?
- Describe how the action increases as the plot moves toward the story's climax.
- Write a modern-day dramatization of this story.

2. During biblical times, it was commonly believed that there was a connection between a person's sin and illness. In present times, we tend to think of "sin" as doing something wrong. John 9:1-41 doesn't define sin in either of these ways. Instead, John uses the literary tool of redefining theological words for the community through Jesus' presence and actions.

- Where do you see the theme of sin in this story?
- How is judgment part of the story?

Bonus Activity:

Being cast out of the synagogue and torn from their religious roots would have made the Jewish Christians a minority community. Such communities often make sense of their new identity through storytelling and the creation of new rituals or means by which to tell the story. One example of using stories to redefine and celebrate group identity is Kwanzaa. Create a Kwanzaa display and describe the purpose behind the celebration. Light the candles and invite learners to compare the reasons the African American community created and celebrates Kwanzaa with the situation of the community of John. Encourage reflection based on the totality of the group's exploration of John thus far.

Tip:

You can find background information on Kwanzaa at http://www.officialkwanzaawebsite.org/index.shtml. If you choose to use candles, check your local fire codes and your congregation's fire polices regarding the use of open flames.

Tip:

Ask the group if they know of any other minority communities that have recreated their stories and rituals in order to develop a deeper understanding of their identity in the wider culture.

Bonus Activity:

Do an online search at a site like www.textweek.com to locate pictures of Jesus healing people. Create a visual display of these pictures in your meeting area. Play soft music and invite learners to meditate on the pictures of Jesus for a few minutes. Invite them to journal their reflections on Jesus and healing. Share reflections if time permits.

Tip:

Look up "rising action" on the Internet prior to the class session to get a better idea of how this term is used by writers.

SESSION FOUR

 Bonus Activity:
Break into trios and give each group a piece of chart paper and markers. Invite the groups to diagram or draw a depiction of the intense drama of this story. Reconvene in the larger group and share the drawings. What similarities and differences do you notice?

 Tip:
Break into pairs or trios and give paper and pens to each group. Consider sharing these dramatizations in Sunday school or worship.

 Bonus Activity:
Form two groups. Assign each group one of two words: *sin* or *judgment*. Ask the groups to discuss their views and definitions of *sin* or *judgment*. How are these similar or different from John's views and definitions? Create dramatizations of the assigned words based on the definitions in the Gospel of John.

 Bonus Activity:
Form pairs and invite them to illustrate or depict in some visual way their interpretation of John's definition of the word *judgment*. Learners can do this by drawing on chart paper, using clay or other modeling material, or by creatively using items found throughout the room.

 Tip:
Consider bringing a variety of interesting objects to the session that learners might creatively use for this activity.

Lutheran Context

1. Use the Lutheran principle of Scripture interprets Scripture to learn more about what "judgment" means in the Gospel of John. What does each of the following passages say about judgment? How do these passages help you better understand John's unique perspective?
- John 3:19-21
- John 5:22-30
- John 16:8-11

2. Lutherans often speak about the law and gospel. The law places demands and expectations on us. The gospel communicates God's love, forgiveness, and promise.
- Review John 9:1-41 and list where you hear demand/law and where you hear promise/gospel.
- How does this text reflect the need for both law and gospel?

Devotional Context

1. Reflect on John 9:1-41.
- What thoughts and feelings do you have about the story of the healing of the blind man?
- If you created a painting about the session Scripture text, what would you include in it?

2. Consider where you might fit in the story, and how God is speaking to you through Scripture today.
- In the story of the healing of the blind man, which person do you identify with the most? Why?
- What is God calling you to see or to do through this story?

Wrap-up

1. Return to the discussion started with the Focus Activity. What makes it difficult for us to see Jesus?

2. Briefly review today's discussion. List any new questions about the material covered in the session. Solicit volunteers to do further research to share with the group in the next session.

3. Point out any "ah-ha" moments that you noticed in the session. What "ah-ha" moments did learners experience?

4. Point out, or assign, homework for the next session.

SESSION FOUR

Pray

O Gracious God, we give you thanks for loving us so much that you sent your Son, Jesus Christ, into our lives so that he might open our eyes to the wonder and glory of your presence. Thank you for the gifts of new spiritual insights that we receive as followers of Jesus, especially those that we received today during this session. And thank you for all the people you give us to accompany us on this lifelong journey of faith. Amen.

Extending the Conversation (5 minutes)

Homework

1. Read the Scripture text for the next session: John 11:1-44. If time permits, read John 10:1—11:44 (see p. 48 for a daily reading plan).

2. Discover how Jesus redefined the Sabbath day of rest. Read these texts: Matthew 12:1-13; Mark 2:23-28; 3:2-4; Luke 6:1-10; 13:10-17; 14:1-6; John 5:9-18; 7:22-23; 9:14-16.

Looking Ahead

1. Read the Scripture text for the next session: John 11:1-44.

2. Read through the Leader Guide for the next session and mark the portions you wish to highlight for the group.

3. Make a checklist of any materials you'll need to do the Bonus Activities.

4. Continue to pray for members of your group during the week.

Bonus Activity:
Pass out copies of *Evangelical Lutheran Worship*. Ask learners to hunt for a hymn that represents their understanding of the law (demands) expressed in the session Scripture text. Ask them to locate a hymn that represents their understanding of gospel (promise) in the session Scripture text. Discuss the hymn selections.

Bonus Activity:
Role-play the way two people interpret different situations. One person is a person of faith and the other does not accept Jesus. Scenarios might include the sudden illness of a mutual friend; a natural disaster, such as a hurricane; or the daily events of life.

Tip:
Consider breaking into pairs to talk about this question. Reconvene in the larger group for discussion, but don't force sharing.

Tip:
Consider listing "ah-ha" moments on chart paper to refer to at the beginning of the next session during the brief review.

SESSION FOUR

Enrichment

1. If you want a daily plan for reading through the Gospel of John during this unit, read the following sections this week:
   - Day 1: John 10:1-10
   - Day 2: John 10:11-21
   - Day 3: John 10:22-42
   - Day 4: John 11:1-16
   - Day 5: John 11:17-27
   - Day 6: John 11:28-37
   - Day 7: John 11:38-44

2. Visit www.textweek.com, look up John 9:1-41, and review some of the available material.

For Further Reading

Life Lessons: The Gospel of John by Max Lucado (Thomas Nelson, 2006). Provides a journey through the Gospel.

SESSION FIVE

John 11:1-44

Leader Session Guide

Focus Statement

Because of his intimate relationship with God, Jesus has power over life and death, now and for all time.

Key Verse

Jesus said to her, "I am the resurrection and the life. Those who believe in me, even though they die, will live, and everyone who lives and believes in me will never die. Do you believe this?" John 11:25-26

Focus Image

© age fotostock / SuperStock

What Does It Mean that Jesus Is the "Resurrection and the Life"?

Session Preparation

Before You Begin . . .

Take time to consider your thoughts and feelings about what it means to die and be resurrected in and through the power of Jesus Christ. Have you experienced Jesus' power over death in your life? While you are facilitating, listen for new insights being shared by others.

Session Instructions

1. Read this Session Guide completely and highlight or underline any portions you wish to emphasize with the group. Note any Bonus Activities you wish to do.

2. View the Session Prep Video.

3. If you plan to do any special activities, check to see what materials you'll need, if any.

4. Have extra Bibles on hand in case a member of the group forgets to bring one.

Session Overview

HISTORICAL CONTEXT

You'll examine Old Testament Jewish **apocalypticism** to get a deeper understanding of Jesus' conversation with Martha as it appears in John 11:17-27. In this passage, Jesus proclaims that he is "the resurrection and the life." This is an identity that would have been especially meaningful to Martha because of the Jewish beliefs about the end of time and what would happen. This endtime is most clearly described in Daniel 12:1-13, which is the only text in the Old Testament that specifically addresses the resurrection of the dead. It says that the angel Michael will usher in the time of judgment when some of the dead will be raised, while others will be condemned. When Martha says that she knows her brother will be raised at the end of time, she is referring to Daniel's description of what will happen when good clashes with evil at the end of time. Jesus' words, however, go beyond what is described in Daniel. Jesus has the power to grant eternal life now and for all time. By believing in him, a person is connected

Session 5: John 11:1-44   47

SESSION FIVE

> **? Apocalypticism:**
> The belief that the world will end violently in a cosmic clash between good and evil.

to God. So his gift of eternal life is both for the present and for the future.

It was a common belief in biblical times that the soul hovered over the body of a deceased person for three days and that during this period there was a possibility for a resurrection. However, on the fourth day the soul left, eliminating any possibility of regaining life. The fact that Jesus remained where he was for two days longer and did not arrive in Bethany until the fourth day is an indication that Lazarus was really dead, with no hope of recovery. Your group will reflect upon what this may mean in John's telling of this story.

LITERARY CONTEXT

An important literary theme in John's Gospel is Jesus' interaction with women. During biblical times, women held a much lower social status than men. So the fact that Jesus has conversations of great substance with them is noteworthy. Earlier, in John 4, Jesus has a verbal exchange with the Samaritan woman and he tells her that he is the Messiah. John 4:27 tells us that the disciples were surprised by this conversation, but they were afraid to approach Jesus about it. It's also significant that the Samaritan woman carries word of her conversation with Jesus back to her city, and many people come to believe in Jesus as a result.

The raising of Lazarus shows us Jesus' conversations with Martha and then Mary. Martha is the first person to proclaim that Jesus is "the Messiah, the Son of God, the one coming into the world" (John 11:27). Your group will look at the position that women hold in John's Gospel, specifically related to the session Scripture text.

This session focuses on another literary device or tool used by John—the use of "signs." The Gospel of John does not speak of "miracles," as Matthew, Mark, and Luke do. Characters in John instead look for "signs" that Jesus is who he says he is. Through these signs, the other characters in John's Gospel have the opportunity to decide whether they will accept or reject Jesus.

The raising of Lazarus is the climactic sign that takes the Gospel of John to the next level, carrying it from the Book of Signs describing Jesus' ministry to the Book of Glory, in which Jesus will finally be raised and "glorified" on the cross. Your group will examine the use of signs in John, and specifically the raising of Lazarus, as a turning point in the plot of the Gospel.

SESSION FIVE

LUTHERAN CONTEXT

Your group will look at two Lutheran principles of interpreting Scripture. First, you'll use "what shows forth Christ" to explore how this text indicates that the power of eternal life is present through the person of Jesus. Jesus is the Incarnate Word connected with God from the beginning of time. To accept him and his connection with God is to receive the gift of **eternal life** for all time. So, when Jesus raises Lazarus from the dead, he dramatically demonstrates his power over death. It is also a precursor of his own glorification on the cross and his eventual resurrection.

Using the principle of Scripture interprets Scripture, you'll look at the Old Testament text in which Moses encounters God in the burning bush. The story is told in Exodus 3:1-15. Here Moses climbs Mount Horeb and meets God, who instructs him to carry a message to Pharaoh to release the Israelites. Moses asks who shall he say is sending him, and God tells him to say he has been sent by "I AM." This will offer an opportunity to reflect back on your conversation about Jesus' "I am" sayings. When Jesus used the words *I am*, as he does when he calls himself the resurrection and the life, the Jewish Christians would have connected his statement with the calling of Moses.

DEVOTIONAL CONTEXT

Not only is the raising of Lazarus the climax of the first half of John, but it is one of the most dramatic stories in the Gospel. Jesus, knowing that Lazarus is dying, delays his trip to Bethany so that he can show what God's glory and power can do in the face of death and the grave.

You'll look at Jesus' words and actions in this text. How is Jesus the resurrection and the life who gives those who believe in him eternal life, both now and in the future? You'll talk about what this means to you personally. Since this is a passage commonly used in funeral services, learners who have lost close friends and family members may have especially deep ties and reflections on this text. Exploring this will give you the opportunity to get at the heart of John's Gospel and what it means for each of you.

Facilitator's Prayer

Jesus, I don't often think about your power and presence as the "resurrection and the life" in my own life until I encounter the death of a friend or family member. Help me to remember that, even now, because of you I have been transformed and live in the reality and

> **? Eternal life:**
> Being in the presence of Jesus and God, now and for all time.

SESSION FIVE

promise of eternal life. Inspire me and open my ears and heart to the insights shared by other learners as I facilitate this session. May we, together, rejoice in this gift of life that we share in you. Amen.

Gather (10-15 minutes)

Check-in

Ask learners if they want to share any homework completed from the last session or any further insights. If no one chooses to share, give a brief recap of the previous session.

Tip: Come prepared to share some insights you've had over the past week about the last session or any others. Share how these insights have affected your faith or changed you.

Pray

Invite participants to write a brief prayer request on a slip of paper and place their requests in a designated prayer basket. Pass the basket and ask each person to draw a slip of paper and pray the petition aloud. (The requests will be anonymous, so it doesn't matter if participants draw their own.)

Or pray this prayer:

Almighty God, your Son came into the world to free us all from sin and death. Breathe upon us the power of your Spirit, that we may be raised to new life in Christ and serve you in righteousness all our days. Amen. (Adapted from *ELW*, p. 28)

Tip: An alternative is to collect the petitions yourself and pray the prayer.

Focus Activity

Look at the Focus Image. What does it say about life and death? Tell about a time when your life, or the life of someone you know, was renewed and transformed.

Open Scripture (10-15 minutes)

Bring in an audio version of the NRSV Bible (some even have sound effects to play up the dramatic readings). Play the recording as everyone reads along in their own Bibles.

Go to a different place to hear the passage—outside, in a small dark room, or in a basement stairwell leading to a darkened hallway. Stage a creative change of venue that appropriately supports the drama of the reading.

Tip: Look for a location in or around your building to simulate a tomb. If your church is located next to a cemetery, consider introducing the text by a crypt or large memorial stone.

Read John 11:1-44.

- What did you find most surprising about the text?
- What image is most memorable?
- What intrigued you?

Join the Conversation (25-55 minutes)

Historical Context

1. In the Old Testament, the only clear reference to "the resurrection of the dead" is found in Daniel 12:1-13. Martha's response to Jesus in John 11:27 was undoubtedly based on her familiarity with the Jewish beliefs about the end of time in Daniel. Read Daniel 12:1-13.

- How was Martha's response influenced by Jewish beliefs about the end-time found in Daniel?
- How does Jesus' proclamation that he is "the resurrection and the life" challenge traditional Jewish beliefs?

2. In biblical times, many people held the belief that a dead person's soul hovered over the body for three days before departing on the fourth. They thought there was the possibility of a resurrection until the fourth day.

- List reasons why Jesus might have waited until the fourth day to go to Lazarus.

Literary Context

1. Imagine that you are watching Jesus raise Lazarus after he had been dead for four days.

- How would you feel watching this incredible drama unfold before you?
- What would surprise you most?

2. In biblical times, women had lower social status than men. Only children were lower. John's Gospel, however, portrays Jesus' interaction with women who play significant roles in the encounters, acting as witnesses to Jesus' identity.

- Read John 4:1-42 and 20:1-18. What role does each woman have in the story?
- What role does Martha play in John 11:17-27?
- Role-play a conversation between the Samaritan woman, Martha, and Mary Magdalene about their respective conversations with Jesus.

Bonus Activity:

Pass out copies of the explanation of the Third Article of the Apostles' Creed found in Luther's Large Catechism (*Book of Concord*, pages 438:57-439:62). Break into trios and discuss what the Catechism says about death and resurrection. List the similarities and differences between Daniel, John, and the Catechism. What do you notice? Why might that be?

Bonus Activity:

A historical approach to any text requires you to ask "who, what, where, why, when" questions in order to get a better idea of the context. Break into trios and ask participants to read John 11:1-44 and look for "who, what, where, why, when" questions that they'd like to learn more about to better understand the text. Ask for volunteers to do some historical research to be shared at the next session.

Bonus Activity:

Discuss what the Samaritan woman, Martha, and Mary Magdalene learned from Jesus about his identity and his power over death.

SESSION FIVE

3. Chapters 1–12 in the Gospel of John are known as the "Book of Signs" in which God's Incarnate Word, Jesus, reveals himself through signs. Characters in the story then make the decision whether or not they believe in Jesus as a result of observing the sign. Chapters 13–21 are known as the "Book of Glory," which tells of Jesus' glorification on the cross and return to God. Read John 11:45-53.

- How might the story of the raising of Lazarus be a climax and turning point between the two books?
- Describe the reaction of the chief priests and Pharisees to Jesus' signs.

Lutheran Context

1. Start with the Lutheran principle of "what shows forth Christ." Consider all the ways that the session Scripture text points us to a better understanding of Christ's power and presence.

- List the things the text tells us about Christ. How do these things invite us to more fully participate in a relationship with Christ?

Bonus Activity:

Do an Internet search for pictures related to the signs Jesus performed in the first half of the Gospel of John. Set up a display and ask learners to walk around and look at the pictures. Ask them to reflect upon what the images say about Jesus' presence and power. Reconvene as a group and discuss which images had the greatest impact and why.

2. Now use the Lutheran principle of Scripture interprets Scripture. Read Exodus 3:1-15 to shed light on the session Scripture text.

- How, and by what name, is God described in the Exodus text? How, and by what name, is Jesus described in John 11:1-44?
- Compare the Exodus text with John 11:1-44 in more detail. What moves God and Jesus to respond to the situations in each text? Who has objections to what God and Jesus plan to do, and why?
- How might the Exodus text help you better understand Jesus' "I am" sayings, especially the one in this text?

Bonus Activity:

Here's another activity that uses Scripture to interpret Scripture. Matthew, Mark, and Luke all share a story of Jesus raising a little girl from the dead. Form three groups and have each group look up one of the following passages: Matthew 9:18-26; Mark 5:21-43; and Luke 8:40-56. Chart how each of these stories is similar to the raising of Lazarus in John. How are they different? What does this tell you about what John might have been saying about Jesus' power over death?

Devotional Context

1. Imagine that you are in the crowd watching Jesus raise Lazarus after he had been dead for four days.

- What would you be thinking? How would you feel watching this incredible drama unfold before you?

2. John 11:1-44 is a text frequently used in funeral services.

- Why do you suppose this is the case? How would you feel about hearing this text at a funeral service?

Bonus Activity:

A significant theme in the Gospel of John is Jesus' relationship with God even before the beginning of time. Jesus' power and glory are God's power and glory represented through him. Break into pairs. Give each pair a piece of chart paper and some markers. Ask pairs to draw a picture that describes the relationship of the Exodus text to the John text, the relationship of God's power to Jesus' power. Share the drawings and the reasons behind them.

3. God speaks to us through the Bible.

- What does it mean to you that Jesus is the resurrection and the life? What does it mean to your family? To the church?

- What is God saying to you through the story of Jesus raising Lazarus from the dead?

Wrap-up

1. Ask participants what they thought were the highlights of today's session. Point out any "ah-ha" moments you noticed in the session. What "ah-ha" moments did learners experience? What did they find most meaningful in the discussion of the meaning of this text and of Jesus' power over death? Why?

2. Ask participants to reflect upon these questions: What things surprised them, and why? What things intrigued them, and why?

3. List any new questions about the material covered in the session. Solicit volunteers to do further research to share with the group.

4. As the session draws to a close, ask learners to think about how they have been transformed by this session. What might that transformation mean for their daily living?

5. Point out, or assign, homework for the next session.

Pray

Loving God, we give you thanks for expressing your power and presence through your Son, Jesus Christ, who truly is the resurrection and the life. He first conquered death by raising Lazarus from the grave. Then on the cross he showed your glory and three days later conquered death again, and for all time. We thank you that, through Jesus, we too experience both the present reality and future promise of the gift of eternal life. Help us to live daily in the light of this promise. In Jesus' name we pray. Amen.

 Bonus Activity:

Role-play a conversation between two people in the crowd who have just witnessed Jesus raising Lazarus from the dead. What did each see from his or her own perspective? What did they experience as they watched? What do they think about Jesus and his power over death?

Extending the Conversation

Homework

1. Read the Scripture text for the next session: John 13:1-35. If time permits, read all of John 11:45—13:35 (see p. 56 for a daily reading plan).

2. Create a visual presentation of your reflections on this passage. You might consider using photography, drawing, or a clay medium. Be creative!

SESSION FIVE

Tip:
Have a variety of Bible translations on hand so that learners can borrow them. Check the church library to see what is available at the church.

Tip:
Remind those who volunteer to do historical research that they'll be sharing what they find at the next session. Tell them that not all of our contemporary questions can be answered through historical research, so it's okay to simply report back on what they find.

3. Journal your thoughts about this week's session. What new insights did you discover?

4. Read and compare John 11:1-44 from a variety of Bible translations. How are they similar? How are they different? What new insights does this comparison give you?

Looking Ahead

1. Read the Scripture text for the next session: John 13:1-35.

2. Read through the Leader Guide for the next session and mark portions you wish to highlight for the group.

3. Make a checklist of any materials you'll need to do the Bonus Activities.

4. Continue to pray for members of your group during the week.

Enrichment

1. If you want a daily plan for reading through the Gospel of John during this unit, read the following sections this week:
    Day 1: John 11:45-57
    Day 2: John 12:1-11
    Day 3: John 12:12-26
    Day 4: John 12:27-43
    Day 5: John 12:44-50
    Day 6: John 13:1-20
    Day 7: John 13:21-35

2. Do an Internet search at www.youtube.com on "I am the resurrection and the life." Check out a couple of the videos. What did you discover?

For Further Reading

Available from www.augsburgfortress.org/store:

Great Women of the Bible: In Art and Literature by Joe H. Kirchberger and Dorothee Soelle (Fortress Press, 2006). Presents stories and images of 15 women in the Bible, including Mary and Martha.

Lazarus, Mary, and Martha: Social-Scientific Approaches to the Gospel of John by Philip F. Esler and Ronald Piper (Fortress Press, 2006). Studies the Lazarus story and includes full-color illustrations from catacombs.

SESSION SIX

John 13:1-35

Leader Session Guide

Focus Statement
Jesus gives us the new commandment to love one another. Through love and service to our neighbor, we are recognized as his disciples.

Key Verse
I give you a new commandment, that you love one another. Just as I have loved you, you also should love one another. John 13:34

Focus Image

© 2003 Augsburg Fortress

What Does It Mean to Be a Disciple of Jesus?

Session Preparation

Before You Begin...

Take some time to reflect on what it means to be a disciple of Jesus. How hard is it to follow Jesus' command to love if you fear or even dislike your neighbor? As always, be open to the Holy Spirit as you facilitate this session and wait to see what new insights your group will discover together.

Session Instructions

1. Read this Session Guide completely and highlight or underline any portions you wish to emphasize with the group. Note any Bonus Activities you wish to do.

2. View the Session Prep Video.

3. If you plan to do any special activities, check to see what materials you'll need, if any.

4. Have extra Bibles on hand in case a member of the group forgets to bring one.

Session Overview

HISTORICAL CONTEXT

Your group will explore two historical/sociological aspects of Jesus washing the feet of the disciples. First, foot washing was a common practice in Jesus' day. Not only did people wear sandals, but the roads and streets were dusty and dirty. This meant they often walked through manure and other waste on their journeys. So, it was not unusual for guests to have their feet washed when they entered a home for a meal. This act was generally performed by a servant, not by a host. Jesus, as a leader, was definitely not following tradition when he washed the feet of his disciples.

In *Social Science Commentary on the Gospel of John*, Bruce Malina and Richard Rohrbaugh point out a possible deeper meaning to this act. The Mediterranean people of biblical times believed that each person had three bodily "zones of interaction." These included the eyes-heart, the mouth-ears, and the hands-feet. The latter zone was believed to be "the zone of purposeful action [and] is the zone of external behavior or interaction with the

SESSION SIX

environment. It is the zone of doing, performing, making" (p. 223). Therefore, the authors suggest that foot washing washes off the effects of one's actions or behavior. If this were the case, a foot washing could be seen as an act of forgiveness, and therefore would carry a much deeper symbolic meaning as Jesus starts his journey to the cross.

Literary Context

Love is a theme woven throughout the session Scripture text and the last half of the Gospel. In this text, Jesus demonstrates his love for his disciples by washing their feet. In doing so, he sets an example for them. The love theme is more clearly drawn out in John 13:31-35, as Jesus admonishes his disciples to live in the light of the love that he has clearly demonstrated. Love becomes both a blessing and a commandment for the followers of Jesus. Your group will look at the theme of love and how it is woven throughout the session Scripture text.

In John 12:4, Judas Iscariot questions Jesus about Mary's use of costly oil to anoint Jesus' feet. Judas embodies the **antithesis** of the theme of love expressed in John 13:1-35. Once Judas receives the piece of bread from Jesus, "Satan entered into him" (John 13:27). In literary terms, this makes Satan the **antagonist** of the story while Jesus is the **protagonist**. Your group will explore the meaning of the character of Judas and his actions as the antithesis of love.

Lutheran Context

There are strong connections between John 13:1-35 and Martin Luther's interpretation of Christian vocation as the way in which a person lives out his or her baptism in daily life. An important aspect of this concept is the call to love and serve one's neighbor by every means possible. In "An Open Letter to the Christian Nobility of the German Nation," Luther states, "And every one by means of his own work or office must benefit and serve every other, that in this way many kinds of work may be done for the bodily and spiritual welfare of the community, even as all members of the body serve one another" (Project Wittenberg). Your group will explore the session Scripture text in light of this Lutheran understanding of **vocation.**

You'll also use the Lutheran principle of Scripture interprets Scripture to gain deeper insights into the session Scripture text. You'll look at John 15:12-17, in which Jesus speaks about the fruit that he wants his disciples to bear—to love one another as he has loved them. Here he also speaks about the depth of the love he has for them, even to the point of laying down his life. You'll

---

? Antithesis:
The opposite of something.

? Antagonist:
A character who opposes another character, especially the protagonist.

? Protagonist:
The main character in a story.

? Vocation:
Your calling in life, and how you live out your baptism in all aspects of life, including work, home, and leisure.

also examine 1 John 3:18-24 and 4:7-21 to see what this book says about Christian love.

DEVOTIONAL CONTEXT

From a devotional perspective, John 13:1-35 is rich in both the imagery of Jesus washing his disciples' feet and the example of love he sets for his followers through this action. The command for Jesus' disciples to love one another as he loves them is a call to action for every Christian. Your group will explore what loving one another looks like today in daily living. How have you experienced Christ's love from others? How hard is it to love when dealing with a "difficult" person or situation?

Your group will also reflect on the session Scripture text using the T.R.I.P. method for devotional reading or Bible study. This method can be used with other Scripture passages as well.

Facilitator's Prayer

O Loving Jesus, sometimes I find myself judging others, and it's hard to follow your command to love. I forget that judgment is not mine to make and that you call us to love and serve all neighbors, those around the corner and those around the world. As I facilitate this session, open me to the insights that will be shared, so that they will transform me and the other learners to more fully live out your commandment to love. Amen.

Gather (10-15 minutes)

Check-in

Ask learners if they want to share any homework completed from the last session or any further insights. If no one chooses to share, give a brief recap of the previous session.

Pray

O loving God, we thank you for both the gift and the opportunity that living as disciples of Christ offers us. We ask that as we read and discuss today's Scripture text, your Holy Spirit might awaken us to your call to love and serve our neighbors everywhere. Ignite in us a passion to do so in new and creative ways so that through us and our actions, the world might come to truly know you. In Jesus' name we pray. Amen.

Focus Activity

Draw a picture of what it means to you to be a disciple of Jesus.

Tip:
Pass out a piece of paper to each learner and ask each one to draw a picture of what it means to be a disciple of Jesus. (Have a variety of markers, crayons, and colored pencils on hand for this activity.) Take time for learners to share these pictures and explain why they drew what they drew. Consider hanging up the drawings around the room so you can refer to them throughout the session.

SESSION SIX

Open Scripture (10-15 minutes)

Read John 13:1-35.

Solicit two or more volunteers who will reenact the foot washing as the text is read. Encourage someone to act out the part of Peter as those passages are read.

Place a basin of water, a towel, and a candle in a central place in the room. Ask learners to meditatively focus their attention on these items as the text is read.

1. What phrase did you find most memorable?

2. What do you wonder about?

3. What feelings does this text elicit?

Join the Conversation (25-55 minutes)

Historical Context

1. In biblical times, foot washing was a common practice. People generally wore sandals, and the roads and streets were dusty and dirty, so it was not unusual for guests to have their feet washed when they entered a home for a meal. This act was generally performed by a servant, not by a host. Jesus, as a leader, definitely wasn't following common practice when he washed the feet of his disciples.

- What might the act of washing the feet of his disciples say about Jesus?
- Why do you suppose this act surprised Peter?

2. In the Mediterranean culture of Jesus' day, the hands and feet were believed to be the "zones of purposeful action" (*Social Science Commentary on the Gospel of John*, Bruce Malina and Richard Rohrbaugh). It was through the hands and the feet that a person acted on the environment, positively or negatively. The foot washing in the session Scripture text, then, could be seen as an act of forgiveness, washing off the effects of the disciples' actions or behaviors.

 Tip: Be sure to bring a basin and towel. Set up the room with three or more chairs in a prime spot where all can see the action. If you choose to use a candle, check your local fire codes and your congregation's fire policies regarding the use of open flames.

 Tip: Consider soliciting volunteers prior to the session so that they can dress appropriately for this activity.

 Bonus Activity: Look at other examples of foot washing in the Old Testament. Read Genesis 18:1-5; 19:1-3; 24:28-33; 43:24-25. What do these passages tell you about the common practice of foot washing in biblical times? Compare these texts with John 13:1-35. What are the similarities and differences?

 Bonus Activity: Reflect upon the many ways that feet can be "zones of purposeful action" and act upon the environment both positively and negatively. Then paraphrase John's story of the foot washing from the perspective of the feet being the "zones of purposeful action." How does reinterpreting the text from this perspective change its message and meaning for you?

SESSION SIX

- If we view the foot washing in this way, could anyone besides Jesus have washed away the dirt of the disciples' interaction with their environment? Why or why not?
- What might it mean for the disciples to wash one another's feet?

Literary Context

1. In John's Gospel, love for one another is a true mark of discipleship, or a sign of being a follower of Jesus.

- List verses in which love is mentioned or demonstrated in John 13:1-35.
- Is love a blessing, a commandment, or both, for disciples of Jesus?

2. In previous sessions, we have seen several literary devices at work in the Gospel of John. In John 13:1-35, another literary tool comes in. Judas Iscariot and his actions are the *antithesis*, or exact opposite, of the theme of love expressed in this passage. The sharp contrast between Judas's actions and Jesus' actions makes the love shown by Jesus stand out even more.

- How is the character of Judas in this story the exact opposite of love?
- Judas is the one disciple who does not receive the commandment to love. Why might that be?
- Who might be behind Judas's actions, and why?

Bonus Activity:

The words *love* and *commandment* seem to be opposing words. Reflect upon how and why Jesus commands his disciples to love one another. Next, dramatize a conversation between two people in which one person is trying to explain to another how and why Jesus can call love a commandment.

Lutheran Context

1. Lutherans place a strong emphasis on the concept of *vocation*, or the living out of baptism in all aspects of life, including work, home, church, and leisure. This call has a strong community orientation. Through our work and various activities, we love, serve, and respect our neighbor. Our "neighbors" include family, friends, coworkers, and strangers.

- How is this Lutheran concept of vocation related to John 13:1-35?
- Make a list of ways to love one another and live out the baptismal call in the workplace, at home, in the congregation, and in leisure activities.

2. Using the Lutheran principle of Scripture interprets Scripture, delve deeper into what it means to be a disciple of Jesus. Read and discuss the following passages: John 15:12-17; 1 John 3:18-24; and 1 John 4:7-21.

- What do these texts say about being Jesus' disciple?

Bonus Activity:

Break into pairs. Give each pair a piece of chart paper and a marker. Tell learners that the Lutheran concept of vocation includes things like family relationships and roles, the role of friend, church involvement, educational pursuits, and community service. List the different vocations that each person is currently living out in his or her life. Reconvene in the large group and share the lists.

Session 6: John 13:1-35   59

SESSION SIX

Bonus Activity:
Pass out copies of *Evangelical Lutheran Worship*. Instruct learners to turn to hymn 708, "Jesu, Jesu, Fill Us with Your Love." Sing or read the hymn together. What additional insights does the hymn give about what it means to be a disciple of Jesus?

Bonus Activity:
This session focuses on loving one another as a "mark of discipleship"—something that identifies us as followers of Jesus and helps us to grow in faith. There are many other marks of discipleship. Invite your pastor to talk to the group for a few minutes about marks of discipleship, or what it means in your congregation to be a disciple of Jesus.

Tip:
Refer to page 49 of *Opening the Book of Faith: Lutheran Insights for Bible Study* to learn more about the T.R.I.P. method of Bible study.

Tip:
Try the T.R.I.P. method yourself first. It's easier to explain an activity to others if you've already done it yourself.

- How do these texts contribute to your understanding of John 13:1-35?

Devotional Context

1. Look back at the Focus Image at the start of the session.
- Imagine that you are next in line to have your feet washed by Jesus. How would you feel? What would you say or do?
- When and how have you followed Christ's example of washing feet?
- Has anyone ever served you in this way? Who?
- List new ways that you might express love for your neighbor in daily life.

2. Spend some time discussing what it means to be a disciple of Jesus and what this looks like in daily life.
- Tell about a time you saw or experienced someone loving another as Christ has loved us.
- How hard is it to love when dealing with a "difficult" person or situation?

3. Use the T.R.I.P. method to look at John 13:1-35. (This method, used by Mount Carmel Ministries, is described in *Opening the Book of Faith: Lutheran Insights for Bible Study* by Diane Jacobson, Stanley N. Olson, and Mark Allan Powell, p. 49.)
T = Thanks: What in the text makes me thankful?
R = Regret: What in the text causes me regret?
I = Intercession: What does the text lead me to pray for?
P = Plan of Action: What action does the text encourage me to take?

Wrap-up

1. Take a moment to look back at the drawings from the Focus Activity. Would any drawings change based on new insights discovered in this session? If so, how would they change?

2. Ask learners what they thought were the highlights of today's session. Point out any "ah-ha" moments that you noticed in the session.

3. Ask learners what new insights they have about the Lutheran concept of Christian vocation.

4. List any new questions about the material covered in the session. Solicit volunteers to do further research to share with the group.

SESSION SIX

Pray

Gracious and loving God, we give you thanks that through the gift of baptism and your baptismal call to us, you empower us and call us to love and serve our neighbor. Open our eyes and our hearts so that we might recognize the needs of those around us and around the world. Help us keep the command to love before us at all times. In Jesus' name we pray. Amen.

Extending the Conversation (5 minutes)

Homework

1. Read the Scripture text for the next session: John 17:1-26. If time permits, read all of John 13:36—17:26 (see page 64 for a daily reading plan).

2. Use *The Book of Concord: The Confessions of the Evangelical Lutheran Church* to do some additional reading on the topic of the Lutheran concept of vocation. Look up "vocation" in the index. Write a brief summary of what you learn and share it at the next session.

3. Write a poem based on John 13:1-35. Bring it to share at the next session.

Looking Ahead

1. Reflect on how things went during this session. What did you learn about facilitating a Bible study? What worked well? What might you have done differently?

2. Reflect upon the preferred learning styles of your adult learners. What came easier to your group? Do they prefer learning through visual means, conversational means, or through physical activities?

3. Read the Scripture text for the next session: John 17:1-26.

4. Read through the Leader Guide for the next session and mark portions you wish to highlight for the group.

5. Make a checklist of any materials you'll need to do the Bonus Activities.

6. Note next week's Historical Context bonus activity on looking up references to the word *name* in John. (If you can't locate

SESSION SIX

 Tip:
Concordances come in a variety of biblical translations, so be sure you have one that matches the majority of the learners' Bible translations.

multiple concordances, compile a list of references you can copy and hand out in class.)

7. Continue to pray for members of your group during the week.

Enrichment

1. If you want a daily plan for reading through the Gospel of John during this unit, read the following sections this week:
   - Day 1: John 13:36-38
   - Day 2: John 14:1-14
   - Day 3: John 14:15-31
   - Day 4: John 15:1-27
   - Day 5: John 16:1-15
   - Day 6: John 16:16-33
   - Day 7: John 17:1-26

2. If your congregation has a foot-washing service during the year, find out if your group can assist in some way. If your congregation doesn't have a foot-washing service, talk with your pastor about planning one, perhaps for Maundy Thursday (the Thursday before Easter).

For Further Reading

Available from www.augsburgfortress.org/store:

The Call to Discipleship by Karl Barth (Fortress Press, 2003). Discusses what it means to follow Jesus in faith.

The Cost of Discipleship by Dietrich Bonhoeffer (Simon & Schuster, 1996). Focuses on how to follow the teachings of Jesus.

Listen! God Is Calling! Luther Speaks of Vocation, Faith, and Work by D. Michael Bennethum (Augsburg Fortress, 2003). Encourages Christians to connect the resources of faith with the challenges of daily life and work.

Real Faith for Real Life: Living the Six Marks of Discipleship by Michael W. Foss (Augsburg Books, 2004). Invites readers to rely on six time-tested marks of discipleship that encourage the practice of faith in everyday life: daily prayer, Bible reading, weekly worship, Christian service, relationships that encourage spiritual growth, and giving in the spirit of generosity.

SESSION SEVEN

John 17:1-26

Leader Session Guide

Focus Statement

Jesus prays that we may be one with him, with God, and with one another, as we continue his ministry in the world.

Key Verse

As you have sent me into the world, so I have sent them into the world. John 17:18

Focus Image

© age fotostock / SuperStock

How Does Jesus Want His Disciples to Relate to the World?

Session Preparation

Before You Begin . . .

Take some time to reflect upon what it feels like to know that you are part of the believing community that Jesus says God gave to him. How does that transform your thinking about the session Scripture text? How does it feel to know that when Jesus is praying in John 13:31—17:26, he's praying for you, even as you prepare to facilitate this session? As always, remain open to any new insights shared in your group discussion.

Session Instructions

1. Read this Session Guide completely and highlight or underline any portions you wish to emphasize with the group. Note any Bonus Activities you wish to do.

2. View the Session Prep Video.

3. If you plan to do any special activities, check to see what materials you'll need, if any.

4. Have extra Bibles on hand in case a member of the group forgets to bring one.

Session Overview

HISTORICAL CONTEXT

John 17:1-26 is part of a much larger unit known as Jesus' farewell discourse. It begins in John 13:31 and continues through John 17:26. In this farewell discourse, Jesus predicts his death and clearly passes on his mission and his position, or unity, with God to his followers.

Farewell discourses from leaders were not unusual in the ancient Mediterranean world. In addition, it was believed that people who were close to death had prophetic and near divine knowledge of future events and circumstances and could tap into this knowledge because they were also believed to be closer to the heavenly realm than to the earthly realm of existence.

SESSION SEVEN

In a farewell discourse, a leader would often predict his or her death. Then the leader would talk, usually in some detail, about what the future would be like for the followers once he or she was gone. As pointed out in *Social Science Commentary on the Gospel of John*: "In the United States, with economics as the focal social institution, final words and testaments deal with the disposition of goods. In Mediterranean antiquity, however, with the kinship institution being focal, final words deal with concern for the tear in the social fabric resulting from the dying person's departure" (Malina and Rohrbaugh, p. 222). Finally, the farewell discourse would often lay out the dying person's legacy and pass on his or her authority to another.

Other notable farewell discourses include Socrates in *Plato's Apology* (39c), Jacob (Genesis 49:1-28), and Moses (Deuteronomy 31–33).

Your group will look at the historical/sociological form of the farewell discourse, or last words, to see what new insights this sheds on Jesus' words.

From a sociological standpoint, you will also consider the ancient beliefs surrounding the power contained in a name. It was generally believed that when you were given and carried a name, you also carried its power with you. It's significant that Jesus asks God to protect and **sanctify** his followers in God's name. You'll look at the power in a name and how knowing this gives new insights into the passage.

LITERARY CONTEXT

The session Scripture text is written in the literary form of a prayer from Jesus to God. This prayer is known as the "High Priestly Prayer" because it is Jesus' prayer of intercession to God on behalf of his disciples, prior to his death on the cross. The prayer has three parts. First, Jesus prays that God's presence and power might be known through him as his time in the world is drawing to an end (John 17:1-8). Then, he prays for his community of believers that they might be protected as they are sent to carry on Jesus' ministry (John 17:9-19). Finally, he prays for future believers that they, too, might be unified in his name (John 17:20-26). The prayer indicates that the future of the community is to be in God's hands alone. Your group will dissect this prayer to look at its form and progression.

You will also look at John's use of the word *world* in his Gospel. John uses this word more than 70 times in his Gospel, but he's not always using the word the same way. Sometimes he uses it in

> **? Sanctify:**
> To make "holy," also to send out in one's name.

the negative sense to refer to those who oppose Jesus, both the religious authorities and Satan (John 12: 31; 15:18-19; 16:11). Other times he uses *world* to refer to those in Israel who do not yet know and believe in him (John 3:16; 12:19; 12:47). Still other times he uses it to refer to the physical world (John 8:23; 9:5; 9:32; 17:24). Your group will examine the text to discuss John's use of *world*.

Lutheran Context

To answer the question, "How does Jesus want his disciples to relate to the world?" you'll use the Lutheran principle of Scripture interprets Scripture to look at why Jesus came into the world and how and why he related to it. From the start of John's Gospel, it is clear that Jesus is being sent so that those who do not yet know God may believe because of Jesus' signs and witness in God's name. In both John 3:17-19 and 12:44-50, we read that Jesus came into the world as its light, not to condemn the world but to save it. In John 15:26-27, Jesus tells his community of followers that they will be empowered by the Holy Spirit to witness to the world in his name. In the High Priestly Prayer, Jesus turns over his mission to his disciples and asks God to protect and guide their future ministry.

Lutherans talk about justification by grace through faith. What we mean by this is that we are not saved or justified by anything that we do. Instead, we believe that through Jesus, God has acted on our behalf to forgive us our sins and give us the promise of eternal life.

The Gospel of John places a heavy emphasis on a person's response to Jesus and whether he or she believes. This easily could be misinterpreted to mean that "to be saved, you've just got to believe!" However, that would mean the act of salvation rests with us. You'll look at the session Scripture text again, in light of justification by grace through faith, to see what new insights you gain.

Devotional Context

In the session Scripture text, Jesus prays for the community of believers who have come to know him, and through him have come to know God. Finally, he prays for those who will yet come to believe in him through the work and witness of this community of believers. That means this prayer is for the church throughout the ages, including us!

Unity is a major focus of the text, especially in John 17:20-26. Jesus makes it clear that he and God are one, and believers are

SESSION SEVEN

now also united with God through their belief in him. Jesus also prays that the community of believers might be unified as, together, they face the world and its challenges.

With your group, you'll look at this prayer and its impact: the knowledge that you are part of the community of believers Jesus is praying for. You'll also reflect upon how unity with God and one another through Jesus makes a difference in how you live out your vocation and discipleship in the world today.

Facilitator's Prayer

Jesus, sometimes the world seems to be a bit threatening, and I feel fearful, insecure, and out of place. Yet, I know that you call us to both live and serve in the world, which includes my community and beyond. During my times of fear and uncertainty, reassure and uplift me with the knowledge that your High Priestly Prayer was for me, too. Help me to share that reassurance with those who will participate in this session. Amen.

Gather (10-15 minutes)

Check-in

Ask learners if they want to share any homework completed from the last session or any further insights. If no one chooses to share, give a brief recap of the previous session.

Pray

Begin the prayer with these words: *"Let us remember these words that Jesus prayed on our behalf."* Then pray John 17:20-24 aloud.

Or pray:

Draw your church together, O God, into one great company of disciples, together following our teacher Jesus Christ into every walk of life, together serving in Christ's mission to the world, and together witnessing to your love wherever you will send us; for the sake of Jesus Christ our Lord. Amen. (ELW, p. 75)

Focus Activity

Reflect on the Focus Image. How does it relate to the previous session? As a disciple of Christ, where are you leaving footprints? Draw a map or picture showing this.

Tip:
Have learners break into pairs for discussion. Reconvene in the larger group and ask for volunteers to share their reflections and maps or drawings.

66   John Leader Guide

SESSION SEVEN

Open Scripture (10-15 minutes)

Read John 17:1-26.

Ask listeners to gravitate toward a single word from the reading that they will later share with the group, along with the reasons why that word remained on their hearts and minds.

Read the passage from several different translations.

1. What word were you drawn to?

2. What did you find most engaging about this text?

3. What confused you?

 Tip:
Reading the passage from several translations is especially helpful with this text. Besides the New Revised Standard Version, consider using the New International Version, Today's English Version, and a children's Bible.

Join the Conversation (25-55 minutes)

Historical Context

1. The session Scripture text is part of a longer speech recorded in John 13:21—17:26, known as Jesus' farewell discourse. Farewell discourses were not unusual in the ancient Mediterranean world. A dying leader would give a speech, similar to a verbal last will and testament, for family and friends. In this speech, the leader might predict his or her death. Relationships and the security of those left behind were generally the main focus, and the dying person's authority or position would be passed on to someone else.

- In John 17:1-26, what provisions does Jesus make for his current disciples after his death?
- What predictions does Jesus make in the text?
- What does Jesus pass on to his disciples?

2. In the ancient world, many people believed that when you carried the name of another, you could draw on the authority and power of the original bearer of the name.

- What does Jesus say in the text about God's name?

Literary Context

1. John 17:1-26 is written in the form of a prayer (known as the High Priestly Prayer) that Jesus prays to God on behalf of his disciples. It can be divided into three major sections: John 17:1-8; 17:9-19; and 17:20-26.

 Bonus Activity:
Form two groups and ask learners to look up the farewell discourses given by two Old Testament leaders: Jacob (Genesis 49:1-28) and Moses (Deuteronomy 31–33). What are the similarities between Jesus' discourse and these other examples? What are the differences?

 Tip:
Before the session, read through both farewell discourses yourself. Consider using Deuteronomy 31, instead of Deuteronomy 31–33, to save time.

 Bonus Activity:
Bring copies of a concordance to the session. Form small groups (each group should have a concordance). Ask the groups to look up other references to the word *name* in John's Gospel. What more do these passages tell you? What new insights does this give you? Reconvene in the large group and compare insights.

Session 7: John 17:1-26   67

SESSION SEVEN

Bonus Activity:
Break into trios and paraphrase this text using the distinct meaning of "world" that you believe was intended by the writer. Reflect on how this gives you new insights into this passage.

Bonus Activity:
Give each learner a sheet of paper along with a variety of markers or colored pencils. Ask each person to pick out an image or word picture from one of the texts they just read and draw a picture of how it relates to the session passage. Share the pictures with the larger group.

Bonus Activity:
Review the text together. Look for who is in charge. Use a whiteboard or chart paper to list all the signs that God is the central actor in the gift of salvation, not humans.

- What is the focus of each of these sections?
- What progressions do you see from one section to another?

2. The word *world* has a variety of meanings in John's Gospel. It can refer to those who oppose Jesus, to those in Israel who do not yet know and believe in him, and to the physical world.

- Describe how John uses the word *world* in different parts of John 17:1-26.
- Does knowing which use of the word the writer intends make a difference in your understanding of the text? Why or why not?

Lutheran Context

1. Use the Lutheran principle of Scripture interprets Scripture to gain additional insights into John 17:1-26. Jesus sends the disciples out into the world to continue his ministry, so it's helpful to take a look at his relationship to the world. Read these texts: John 3:17-19; 12:44-50; and 15:18-27.

- What do these texts say about Jesus' relationship to the world?
- What might these texts suggest about how Jesus wants his disciples to relate to the world?

2. The Gospel of John emphasizes a person's response to Jesus as the determining factor in whether one receives eternal life. From this, it might be easy for us to say, "You've just got to believe!" Lutherans, however, also consider Martin Luther's insight on *justification by grace through faith*, which says we are not saved or justified by anything that we do. Through Jesus, God has acted on our behalf to forgive our sins and give us the promise of eternal life.

- How would you reconcile the emphasis on our response in John's Gospel with Luther's insight on justification by grace through faith?
- Does justification by grace through faith shed additional light on John 17:1-26?

Devotional Context

1. Jesus prays for the early followers who have come to know him, and through him have come to know God. Finally, he prays for those who will yet come to believe in him through the work and witness of the community of believers. This means Jesus' prayer is for the church throughout the ages, including us today!

- What does it mean to you that when Jesus prayed this prayer, he prayed for you, too?

- Write down some names of people or situations in need of your prayers or the prayers of the church.

2. Jesus makes it clear that he and God are one, and he prays that his followers might be united with God through him. Jesus also prays that the community of believers might be united as they face the world and its challenges together.
- How does Jesus' prayer for unity with God and one another affect how you live out your vocation and call to discipleship?
- How does Jesus want his disciples to relate to the world?
- What is God calling you or your congregation to be or to do through this text?
- Journal any further insights you have on John 17:1-26.

Wrap-up

1. Reflect on the Focus Activity's discussion on the relationship of a Christian to the world. What new insights do you have as a result of this session?

2. Ask learners what they thought were the highlights of today's session. Point out any "ah-ha" moments that you noticed in the session.

3. Ask about any new insights learners had about their unity with God and one another through Jesus, and what that might mean for their ministry in his name.

4. List any new questions about the material covered in the session. Solicit volunteers to do further research to share with the group.

Pray

Jesus, sometimes it is hard for us to remember that, as Christians, we are truly one in mission with you and with one another. You have given us one faith and one baptism, which unite us all. Open our eyes to the many ways that we might serve you in the world, both as a congregation and as individuals. Help us to go forth in ministry knowing that all we do is done in the power of your name, Jesus Christ our Lord and Savior. Amen.

Bonus Activity:
Ask learners to use the Swedish Marking Method (see pages 49–50 of *Opening the Book of Faith: Lutheran Insights for Bible Study*) or the symbols listed on page 1553 in *Lutheran Study Bible* (Augsburg Fortress, 2009) to mark this text. (The Swedish Marking Method suggests using "a candle for a new idea, double candle for a verse you want to memorize, an arrow for a verse that relates to a personal experience, and a question mark when something is not clear.")

Tip:
Try one of the marking methods yourself first. It's easier to explain an activity to others if you've already used it.

Bonus Activity:
Break into trios and ask each to write a brief contemporary prayer based on the session Scripture text. Consider hanging the prayers in the room where you meet, or use them to create a devotional booklet for your group. Or you might seek a volunteer to type the prayers into a word processing program. Create a devotional sheet or booklet for each person.

SESSION SEVEN

Extending the Conversation

Homework

1. Read the next session's Bible passage: John 20:11-31.

2. Search your home for an object that reminds you of the insights you have gained from studying John 17:1-26. Bring it to the next session and be ready to share why you picked this object.

3. Borrow a hymnal, check your library of religious music, or do an Internet search through www.textweek.com to look for a hymn or other music that you feel relates to John 17:1-26. If you are a musician, consider recording an instrumental version to bring to the next session.

4. Jesus prayed for his disciples. Do you know of any followers of Jesus who are in need of your prayers? Pray for them this week.

 Tip: It's entirely appropriate to suggest that learners pray for members of the church staff as part of this homework assignment.

Looking Ahead

1. Read the Scripture text for the next session: John 20:11-31.

2. Read through the Leader Guide for the next session and mark portions you wish to highlight for the group.

3. Make a checklist of any materials you'll need to do the Bonus Activities.

4. Continue to pray for members of your group during the week.

Enrichment

1. If you want a daily plan for reading through the Gospel of John during this unit, read the following sections this week:
   - Day 1: John 18:1-11
   - Day 2: John 18:12-27
   - Day 3: John 18:28—19:16
   - Day 4: John 19:17-42
   - Day 5: John 20:1-10
   - Day 6: John 20:11-31
   - Day 7: John 21:1-25

2. Check your church library for any commentaries on the Gospel of John, and use them to continue to explore John 17:1-26 or any of the other session Scripture texts. Consider sharing your insights with the group at the next session.

3. Reflect on your map or drawing from the Focus Activity. Where is God calling you to leave new footprints? Where is God calling your congregation to leave footprints?

For Further Reading

Available from www.augsburgfortress.org/store:

What Is Mission? Theological Explorations by J. Andrew Kirk (Fortress Press, 2006). Introduces the concept of Christian mission.

The Word That Redescribes the World: The Bible and Discipleship by Walter Brueggemann (Fortress Press, 2006). Provides insights on the situation of Christian communities in today's globalized context.

SESSION EIGHT

How Does Jesus' Relationship with His Disciples Continue?

John 20:11-31

Leader Session Guide

Focus Statement
Jesus gives us the Holy Spirit to accompany us as we go forth to witness in his name.

Key Verse
When he had said this, he breathed on them and said to them, "Receive the Holy Spirit." John 20:22

Focus Image

© IMAGEZOO / SuperStock

Session Preparation

Before You Begin . . .

Take a moment to reflect upon your relationship with Jesus. How do you feel the power and presence of his resurrection in your life? Do you feel it on a daily basis? If not, what tends to get in the way? Keep these things in mind as you facilitate this session.

Session Instructions

1. Read this Session Guide completely and highlight or underline any portions you wish to emphasize with the group. Note any Bonus Activities you wish to do.

2. View the Session Prep Video.

3. If you plan to do any special activities, check to see what materials you'll need, if any.

4. Have extra Bibles on hand in case a member of the group forgets to bring one.

Session Overview

LITERARY CONTEXT

The Gospel of John has reached the climax of the story, fulfilling the plot that was summarized in John 3:16: "For God so loved the world that he gave his only Son, so that everyone who believes in him may not perish but may have eternal life." We are now at the **"denouement"** of the story, when all is finally revealed and made clear.

The story of Jesus appearing before Thomas is a key story in the final revelations of the Gospel. Thomas, who had not been present during the first resurrection appearance of Jesus, expressed doubt. He said he needed to see Jesus' physical body in order to believe. But, when Jesus does appear before him, his doubt turns into the bold proclamation: "My Lord and my God!" In case any doubt remained for readers of the Gospel, we hear the words now clearly spoken. This is who Jesus is!

Jesus fulfills another storyline that started in John 14:15-17 when he promises his disciples the gift of the Holy Spirit. He now gives

SESSION EIGHT

? Denouement:
The resolution and final outcome of a story.

? Ossuary:
An urn or box that carries the bones of the dead.

them a new breath of life through his Holy Spirit so that they are empowered for ministry in his name.

Then in John 20:30-31, John circles back to the opening of his Gospel and tells us that the purpose of his book is that we, too, might believe that Jesus is God's Son through whom we receive the gift of eternal life. Now that all has been revealed, we, too, are called to believe and have eternal life in Jesus Christ.

Your group will look at the resolution and the purpose of the story of Jesus in the Gospel of John and seek to obtain new insights from taking this perspective.

Historical Context

You'll look at this text through what occurred in the burial traditions and customs of Jesus' time. Think back to the previous session on the raising of Lazarus when he was placed in a tomb. Burial practices of the time required bodies to be properly prepared with spices, wrapped in burial cloths, and then placed in a tomb to decompose for about a year. It's important to realize that the mourning process lasted throughout this year-long period of time. After decomposition was complete, the bones were prepared and placed in an **ossuary**, and the tomb could be reused by others. Only at this point was the deceased believed to be ready for the resurrection. As a result, if a body disappeared before it could go through this last stage of preparation, it would not be ready for the resurrection.

Typically, it was not until decomposition had occurred that the penalty of death was considered to be paid. And only then could the remains be prepared for deposit in the ossuary for the resurrection. In *Social Science Commentary on the Gospel of John*, the authors state that the fact that Jesus was crucified as a criminal is important in interpreting what transpired in his resurrection: "God supposedly took Jesus directly from last breath to resurrection because there had been no guilt in his flesh. God intervened before the rotting started, hence God overturned the death sentence" (p. 277).

Your group will examine the text based on the beliefs regarding death and burial held during Jesus' time to see what light is shed on possible interpretation.

SESSION EIGHT

LUTHERAN CONTEXT

You'll once again use the Lutheran principle of Scripture interprets Scripture and look through this lens to gain additional insights into the text. Two major passages in the New Testament tell the story of the arrival of the Holy Spirit: John 20:19-23 and Acts 2:1-13. In each of these passages, the Spirit arrives in very different ways. In John's Gospel, Jesus breathes on his disciples on the day of his resurrection and physically gives them the gift of the Holy Spirit. This act is reminiscent of Genesis 2:7 when God breathes life into man at his creation. It fulfills Jesus' promise that the disciples will not be abandoned. Through the Spirit's presence, they maintain their intimate connection with Jesus even after he is gone. Acts 2 verifies that the coming of the Holy Spirit was a significant event in the life of the new church. As in John, the once frightened disciples are now empowered for ministry in Jesus' name. Although the circumstances of the Spirit's arrival are different, the impact is significant in both texts.

In his discussion of the Apostles' Creed in the Small Catechism, Martin Luther says, "I believe that by my own understanding or strength I cannot believe in Jesus Christ my LORD or come to him, but instead the Holy Spirit has called me through the gospel, enlightened me with his gifts, made me holy and kept me in the true faith, just as he calls, gathers, enlightens, and makes holy the whole Christian church on earth and keeps it with Jesus Christ in the one common, true faith" (*Book of Concord*, ed. Kolb and Wengert, 357:6). Your group will reflect upon Luther's interpretation of the action of the Holy Spirit in our lives.

DEVOTIONAL CONTEXT

This passage shows us that an encounter with the risen Christ is indeed transformational. Through Christ's presence, Mary's weeping is turned into joy and Thomas's doubt is turned into a bold proclamation of belief. Through Jesus' gift of the Holy Spirit, disciples who have not physically seen Jesus come to believe in him. Through the Spirit's presence in the Christian community, we, too, are transformed. This is how Jesus' relationship continues with his disciples of all ages—through the Spirit, the Advocate whom he promised.

Your group will reflect upon what it feels like to know that Jesus gave his Holy Spirit to dwell with us, guide us, and open our eyes and our hearts to the power and the presence of the risen Christ in our lives. How do you experience the transformational power of the risen Christ in your life?

SESSION EIGHT

Facilitator's Prayer

Jesus, sometimes I doubt you. I crave proof of the reality of your presence in my life. It is those times when I need to recall the gift of your Holy Spirit. May your Spirit open my eyes to see you at work in the world and in my life. As I facilitate this session, may I be especially aware of the presence of the Spirit with us as we arrive at new insights into faith and life in you. Amen.

Gather (10 minutes)

Check-in

Ask learners if they want to share any homework completed from the last session or any further insights. If no one chooses to share, give a brief recap of the previous session.

Pray

O God of life, you reach out to us amid our fears with the wounded hands of your risen Son. By your Spirit's breath, revive our faith in your mercy, and strengthen us to be the body of your Son, Jesus Christ, our Savior and Lord, who lives and reigns with you and the Holy Spirit, one God now and forever more. Amen. (ELW, p. 33)

Focus Activity

Reflect on the Focus Image. What signs help you find the way on your journey of faith? Who helps you or accompanies you? What do you carry with you?

Tip: Have learners break into trios for discussion. After a few minutes, have everyone reconvene and share reflections in the larger group.

Open Scripture (10-15 minutes)

Read John 20:11-31.

Select volunteers to read the passage as the narrator, Mary Magdalene, Jesus, and Thomas.

Have one person read the text while participants imagine they are one of the characters in the story. Read through the text a second time, with participants imagining themselves as a different character in the story.

Tip: Consider asking people before the session to serve as these readers so they can practice prior to the session.

1. What emotion did you connect with through the text?

2. What about this text do you find most memorable?

3. What do you still wonder about?

Join the Conversation (25-55 minutes)
Literary Context

1. The end of the Gospel of John brings us to the resolution and final outcome of the story, when all is revealed and made clear. The disciples, who frequently misunderstood Jesus in the rest of the Gospel, now understand the significance of his words and actions.
- What signs of resolution do you see in John 20:11-31?
- What promises are fulfilled?
- What new insights are discovered by the characters?

2. The purpose statement of the Gospel appears in John 20:30-31.
- Why do you suppose the writer placed the purpose statement at the end of the book?
- Do you think the writer accomplished this purpose? Why or why not?

Historical Context

1. In biblical times, death was considered to be a much longer process than just the moment of physical death. Typically, after a person died, the body was prepared with spices, wrapped in burial cloths, then placed in a tomb to decompose. After a year, the body was brought out and the bones were placed in an urn or box. The mourning process officially ended at this point. People believed that if a body disappeared before it could go through this last stage of preparation, it would not be ready for the resurrection.
- How might this description of the death and mourning process further explain Mary Magdalene's distress at finding the tomb empty?
- What new insights does this give you into what's happening in John 20:11-31?
- Role-play John 20:11-18. Show Mary Magdalene's distress at finding an empty tomb and her joy at discovering Jesus was alive.

 Bonus Activity:
Create a plot diagram as a group. Plot or list important stories in the Gospel of John. Concentrate on the session Scripture texts. What impact do the individual stories have in John's Gospel?

Tip:
A sample plot diagram can be viewed at http://www.d.umn.edu/~moor0145/plotdiagram.htm. Plot diagrams are based on the Freytag Triangle or Pyramid, developed by Gustav Freytag in 1863.

 Bonus Activity:
Dramatize the disciples explaining to Thomas that Jesus appeared to them, along with Thomas's response. Then dramatize the meeting between Jesus and Thomas. After you've done the dramatization, discuss the role that Thomas plays. What does this character do within John's Gospel?

 Bonus Activity:
Consider doing a first-person presentation that shows Mary reflecting on what it felt like to be at the empty tomb and then later to learn that Jesus was alive.

 Tip:
Solicit volunteers to do the role-play. Afterward, discuss what you experienced as a group witnessing this story.

SESSION EIGHT

Bonus Activity:

Break into small groups and use study Bibles, historical reference books, and commentaries on the manners and customs of biblical times to read more on the death and burial customs of Jesus' day. Ask the groups to share what they learned. What new insights were shed on the text as you learned more about the burial customs of Jesus' day?

Bonus Activity:

Distribute copies of *Evangelical Lutheran Worship*. Ask learners to turn to hymn 407, "O Living Breath of God." Read or sing through the hymn together. Reflect on its words. What might it feel like to have the Holy Spirit breathe through us? What does this mean to you?

Tip:

If no one in your group is musical, ask your choir or music director to record the music to this hymn so you can sing along. Play the hymn through once before the group sings it together.

Tip:

Obtain copies of the Small Catechism and distribute them to learners for this discussion. Have participants turn to the explanation of the Third Article of the Apostles' Creed.

2. According to *Social Science Commentary on the Gospel of John*, the fact that Jesus was crucified as a criminal is important for understanding what happened at his resurrection. A criminal's death penalty typically was not considered to be fulfilled until the body had decomposed.

- What might it mean that God raised Jesus before the death penalty of a criminal would have been fulfilled?

Lutheran Context

1. Using the Lutheran principle of Scripture interprets Scripture, look at two texts that tell about Jesus' disciples receiving the gift of the Holy Spirit after his resurrection: John 20:19-23 and Acts 2:1-13.

- What is each text saying about the gift of the Holy Spirit? How are the texts different?
- How does Acts 2:1-13 help you understand John's version of the arrival of the Holy Spirit?

2. In his explanation in the Small Catechism to the Third Article of the Apostles' Creed, Martin Luther wrote that we can't come to believe in Jesus Christ on our own. Instead, we need the Holy Spirit to both bring us into a relationship with Jesus and to maintain that relationship on a daily basis. Luther says that the Spirit calls, gathers, enlightens, makes us holy, and keeps us in the faith.

- How does this Lutheran approach to understanding the Holy Spirit shed light on the session Scripture text?
- How does the text shed light on Luther's understanding of the need for the Holy Spirit in the life of the believer?

Devotional Context

1. An encounter with the risen Christ has the power to transform or change us. Through Christ's presence, Mary's weeping is turned into joy and Thomas's doubt is turned into a bold proclamation of belief.

- How has the risen Christ transformed you and your life, or how is the risen Christ transforming you now?

2. With the Holy Spirit to accompany you, Jesus sends you out to continue his ministry in the world.

- How do you feel about this? What does it mean to you personally?
- Through the words of today's Scripture text, what is God calling you to be or to do?

SESSION EIGHT

Wrap-up

1. Reflect on the Bonus Gathering Activity's discussion. Do learners have any new insights now?

2. Ask learners what they thought were the highlights of today's session. Point out any "ah-ha" moments that you noticed in the session. How have learners developed new understandings of John as a result of participating in this study?

3. List any new questions about the material covered in the session. Since this is the last session in this unit, ask how learners might seek answers to these questions.

4. Ask the group for any closing thoughts on this study on the Gospel of John. Share your thoughts as well.

Pray

Gracious and loving God, your love for us is wide and deep. You love us and the world so much that you sent your Son, Jesus Christ, to take on flesh and walk and live among us. Through him, you give us an eternal relationship with you. Empower us, through your Holy Spirit, to celebrate this relationship and share your love with those nearby and around the world. In Jesus' name we pray. Amen.

Extending the Conversation (5 minutes)

Homework

1. Consider what Bible studies you might pursue next in the Book of Faith initiative.

2. God sends the Holy Spirit to draw us into relationship with Christ and help us grow in faith each day. Write a poem on what it means for you to have a relationship with Jesus Christ through the presence of the Holy Spirit in your life.

Looking Ahead

1. Reflect back on this Bible study and how things went during each session. What did you learn about facilitating a Bible study? What worked well? What might you have done differently?

 Bonus Activity:
Create several stations around the room with pictures or symbols that represent the Holy Spirit. Play meditative music and invite learners to silently visit the stations and reflect upon the Holy Spirit's presence. What does it mean to know that through the Spirit we come to know Christ and maintain our lifelong journey of faith with him? Offer an opportunity for learners to journal their thoughts.

 Tip:
Do an Internet search on the Holy Spirit to get ideas for the stations. You might also include a candle at one station. Bring in a small fan; attach red, orange, and yellow streamers; and turn it on.

 Tip:
Consider Gregorian chants or Native American flute music for background music. If you choose to use a candle, check your local fire codes and your congregation's fire polices regarding the use of open flames.

 Bonus Activity:
Give learners lumps of clay to mold and sculpt as they reflect upon what transformation and new life in Christ feels like. Share reactions with the group.

 Tip:
Remind learners to have some fun with this, too. They're not expected to produce works of fine art, just express themselves.

2. Reflect upon the preferred learning styles of your adult learners. What came easier to your group? Did they prefer learning through visual means, conversational means, or through physical activities?

3. Consider what studies you might pursue next in the Book of Faith initiative.

4. Continue to pray for members of your group.

Enrichment

1. Obtain a copy of *The Book of Concord: The Confessions of the Evangelical Lutheran Church,* edited by Robert Kolb and Timothy J. Wengert (Fortress Press, 2000). Read and take notes on the explanation of the Third Article of the Apostles' Creed in both the Small and Large Catechisms.

For Further Reading

Available from www.augsburgfortress.org/store:

Resurrection by Alister E. McGrath (Fortress Press, 2007). Explores Christ's resurrection through art, poetry, prayer, and reflection.

www.ingramcontent.com/pod-product-compliance
Lightning Source LLC
Chambersburg PA
CBHW081401290426
44110CB00018B/2451